T0198671

NOT THE BEGINNING, NOR THE END

BRANIMIR BANE MAKSIMOVIC

BALBOA.
PRESS

A DIVISION OF HAY HOUSE

Balboa Press books may be ordered through booksellers or by contacting:

Balboa Press
A Division of Hay House
1663 Liberty Drive
Bloomington, IN 47403
www.balboapress.com.au
1 (877) 407-4847

Print information available on the last page.

ISBN: 978-1-5043-0881-6 (sc)
ISBN: 978-1-5043-0882-3 (e)

Balboa Press rev. date: 06/23/2017

From left, two write, and back again.
Within, are angles, a past, & future.
...The present, its Momentum...

In a world where there are no secrets, and a place where there is so much pain, in a life where so much can be confusing, and a destiny not many understand, a path many think they know, and mistakes that are not always ours, bodies that people feel they are not always in control of, and minds that are not always felt free, hope that few have, and love that many look to bury, hate that everyone can show, some still offer themselves, in hope that all others, find the connection.

How does one make a choice, if being controlled. How does one have free will, if in fear. How is there freedom, if ones mind is forbidden.

One must never contain themselves to only overcome one obstacle. One must never apply themselves to only one problem. This reduces the ability to see.

There is a feeling that most see a need to stick to the game. The problem is though, that most don't even know the game, or its rules.

Everyone has secrets. But so does everything. The problem can arise, when one knows secrets of things, and things keep the secret from one.

Sometimes we have to live in a state of unawareness, which can last a lifetime. But it can always be cured, by maintaining hope all along.

Confession can make you both pure and impure. For the honest truth, will always be different in another's eyes, depending on who you tell.

Sometimes being apologetic is not what is important. Other times, forgiving, is not all that matters.

A wall can be breached. So do not build the wall around you, be the wall. That way, you are always your best defence.

We fail, to succeed. We succeed, to fail. But we have yet to fail successfully enough, so that we are considered a failure.

The neck was designed to turn 180 degrees, so that you would find your opposite, in order to cover the entire 360 degrees of your lives.

At times, there seems to never be an ending in sight. There seems to be only pain along the way. When that seems true, you must search more.

What appears lost, may just be a road, few understand.

Even intelligence requires belief.

What is right, will tend to be wrong, and what is incorrect, will tend to be truth. So does one fight, for justice, or bow down, to an alternate reality.

Reactions, are actions, that are never accepted. Making consequences, irrelevant, when explaining a reaction. Physical Inactivity then becomes right at times.

There is no man, or beast, that has endured pain, and expanded its barrier, like that of few. For what they witness, love is the miracle.

A prayer will always be answered. But one should not always wait for its response. For it arrives, in many forms, and not always how expected.

Self education, will change the modern world, as it changed the old world. But formal education, should not be the only one rewarded, for within itself, self education is what makes it appear extra ordinary.

There is a reality that the entire would can see, but the entire world denies. The effort and sacrifice of many, that has tried to be washed away, yet surfaces back eventually.

Sometimes there is only good in some, without the bad. But the world we live in, interprets anger, and it's consequential reactions, as simply bad. This is a mistake.

We scream religious freedom. Scream freedom of speech. Scream Liberty. But if we scream freedom too loud, then we are only screaming.

The absence of action, can sometimes be the introduction of greater understanding. For not all true revelations can be acted upon, immediately.

There are some minds, that should not always be listened to, because they cannot be understood. These minds are governed by emotions too often, but their reality, perhaps delusional for many, is only a greater reality.

Sometimes we write down our hearts through words. Sometimes we show our hearts through actions. But our dreams, are our hearts, in reality.

There is no righteousness, in doing wrong. There is no wrong, in seeking righteousness.

If we abandon, that which is far from our reach, then we forget, how far we have already progressed.

Shed a tear, not from fear, but what you hear, from your peer. Do it right, keep insight, what's rarely bright, yet shines delight, to find the light.

It is true that we see what we wish to see, if the word wish is used without meaning. Some can see a wish, that can be true to all. Most can only see, what no one wishes nor is true.

What is a great man, without a great woman. Just a man, without complete greatness.

It is important to understand the difference between simply hating, and hating something. Without hating what is wrong, you cannot love what is good.

We tend to regret something once it's too late, mainly due to our lack of belief. But believe, that the other side, will rarely feel regret.

In life we wait for many things, and patience is the most prevalent response. But unlike a few things, time will not wait for anything.

It always comes down to intelligence, at one point or another.

A wolf will howl, a lion will roar, a snake will hiss. But when the sky rumbles, they will all bow down with absolute respect. As all things, the creatures teach a path.

When you hear the cry of the birds, do not listen only with your ears, but listen to the direction they fly, and the way they move.

We all face different challenges. We all face different forms of injustice. But we are not all faced, with a multi-faced reality.

We use it to breath, to give life to the water, the source for every reaction on earth, it is in essence, the formidable power, it is the air.

If we search for the golden middle, we must move forward little by little, coming across every fiddle, working it out through the riddle.

You may not find what your were looking for, or perhaps you were not searching. So let life be a mystery at times, so that it's protected.

Never let deceit, or that which you cannot change, Drain the energy from yourself, so just turn over to the next page, and return upon the last, when you reach that stage.

When love is seen through the eyes, there is no need for a word.

There is no balance, and compromise is hard on earth. There is only will, to try and balance, what has rarely found compromise.

The vast majority of humanity, will forever live a life, surrounded by a few lies and uncertainty. Few will live a lie, because of humanities unawareness.

Most hearts are half broken & half full of love. The hearts won over by the broken side, may be ruled by negativity. The other side, heals everything.

A glimpse of genius, has the power to show ones true colours. A requirement of living like a fool, may show the true colours of those around.

We are but 1, divided in oneness, causing a whole, to become multiple ones, causing division, within the truth, to becoming, the power of 1.

Stability, a word, so loosely based on the physical world, so misunderstood in the psychological realm. Thus becoming, open to perception.

Perfection exists. In an action, a response, a movement, a law, for us to exist, in words. Imperfection only exists, because of difference.

Truth has a different face for everyone. Some base it on experience, interest, selectivity. Those that base it on reality, should not be considered delusional.

Unfortunately, for the greater good of peace and order, entire truths will never be told on time, and few will be demonised, for many to feel good.

That candy can only be taken from the child, if the child is not protected. If it is taken then, it will always be taken from the adult also.

Where few know, many who desire to know, yet, cannot, fail all.

We all scream freedom. We all yell Liberty. But we all, yes, we all, take it away from at least one other, but few remember to return it, that is the problem.

We seek to recreate a virtual world. For so many reasons. It would provide safety, freedom, and life. Unlike the current reality for too many.

There is no place like home. No place like Earth. No thing like life. There is no place to hide. No place to go. There is no other existence.

Humanity is a testimony to itself. No oath can be unbroken. No world can be brought down. It's time for humanity to give a new testimony.

People can be like gravity. Always pulling someone down. This is easily defied.

Hope, when all seems hopeless. Believe, when everyone gives up. Fight, when all is defeated. Love, when only hate presides. Never give up.

The heart can not send the true feeling to a thought. The thoughts can be manipulated with the words. The words, will then, affect the heart. But the energy, reveals the entire part.

We are all in control of our lives, but we have all become out of control with the way we live.

No one is limited. But not all reach their true height.

Approach can change. Style can differ. Selection will alter. But the essence of what is, what can be, and what shall be, will stay the same.

The universe is too large for itself to be aware of its own vastness of information. But if it's there, it is always accessible. But by whom.

Intuition can be deceiving. But do not try to deceive your own intuition. You will only deceive yourself.

Paganism was once religion. Beliefs turned into religion. Traditions moulded into religions. But faith, has and forever will be faith.

Leap for that which no one has before. Reach out for that which seems too far. Love so much that it appears stupid. Pray, as if you're alone.

Write to set your soul free. Free yourself to write soulfully. Use your soul to write freely.

There is not a plant, a chemical, an object, a device, a body, that can do, that which the will of a good spirit can defy.

Who sees what we see, when you're free and me, when our branch is from the first tree, do you still see, what I see, or only see, what you see.

The majority will always win. Life on earth is just a fraction of a fraction of the universe. Earth is the minority, Love is the majority.

Only a blind man will not see what he can hear, but a man with sight, will rarely hear what he can see.

To relinquish what is lost, is difficult surrounded by those who do not know what they are losing

Love will not always be the only solution to some problems. A heart is also required. A heart that understands what love cannot always see.

Thinkers think the thoughts not thought, while also thinking through the thoughts already thought. But thinking freely is clearing through empty thoughts.

One day, perhaps not far from now, humanity will realise, with what ever positive influence provided, humanity shaped their own past & future.

We don't all live. Because we don't all help. We don't all die. Because through help, one immortalises themselves within existence.

Will, will save a life. Will, will save the lives of others. Will, will always make mind over matter a reality. Will, cannot be measured.

Hospitality is not something that should be a separate section of education. It should be one of the first components of life.

Unfortunately, sometimes to make great changes for all, you must accept the reality of moving yourself away from all. Sacrifice can be a form of wisdom.

An opinion can be detrimental to ones career. Not because they aren't correct, but because their extra correctness, is all but conventional.

One who prospers in growing their crops, is also the one who helps all else prosper.

Challenge what is conventional at all times. There has been no point in time, when always agreeing, has allowed anything to make progress.

The mind should be viewed as a black hole. It is always pulling in what doesn't matter, and fights to find evidence of what does matter.

Holding onto grudges can only be avoidable if you don't hold onto those who are always causing these grudges.

An anomaly is never a coincidence. An anomaly is both a sign and there for a purpose. We are told they are not meant to occur, but they do!

Never lose your mind because you have been done wrong by. For if that mind learns and stays strong, so too, justice can be brought forward.

A child will suffer profoundly. They will stay strong, never share their pain and grow up. Again though, will it be that adult who suffers, is up to the child within.

Speaking up to injustice is not always recommended. Not because you don't speak the truth, but because it will simply not be accepted.

It is those that keep their pain and injustice within their minds, that will always be accused first, of the wrongs committed against them.

There are many who will endure continual injustice. They can either accept it as normal, or they can fight to prove, it is abnormality.

Find pleasure in that which is simple for your mind. But never simply be, that which is pleasurable for the minds of others.

You must always fight the battle with at minimum the same weapons. Yet wiser, is to believe more, than those, or that, which fights you.

Evil is a cause of ones very own greed, temptation and lies. There is no devil, or demon, that can cause one to be evil but themselves.

There are those who express themselves as though they carry the weight of the world on their shoulders. Then there are those that perhaps share its burden unequally.

He who seeks peace, will always find it.

Never stop fighting for what is right. Never give up, if only you understand. Always remember though, that your life is not the only one.

Justification of injustice, is satisfaction, only for the sorrow soul.

Pray, so not that you hear yourself. But pray, that you become deaf to what you are saying, and open to the message you are receiving. Pray.

In this world, offering kindness, becomes confusing, as we have developed, a self-conscious life. But doing good, is very self-conscious.

Do not ever look down upon yourself, if you have done good upon someone who has preyed upon you. For they, are not aware, with what they play.

Once we were free to dwell in the vastness of a jungle or desert. Today, such a choice, is deemed psychologically unacceptable.

Everyone expects to be told the truth through words. But there have always walked those, who must find the truth through signs and motions.

Advice to an intelligent man will change the world. Otherwise, advice is usually taken as a stab in the back. Even by looking into the eyes.

We all know that not everyone can be pleased. Nor can everyone be satisfied. So then, seek to please and satisfy those who least expect such surprises.

When you have done a world of good, and been judged by the bad moments. Do not exact anger. But remember, to search for that goodness once more.

Don't expect to be rewarded for the feats your own mind has brought into this world. But expect, even if you don't believe, someone can see.

An individual who seeks perfection, will always find it. They will see it through the mind, only because the body was designed imperfect, or yet incapable of realising its own perfection.

The bee desires peace. In return it offers the sweetness of life. But disrespect the peace a bee desires, and it will return sorrow and pain

Someone will stay positive all day long, and do good only to themselves. Someone will appear negative, and only wish to do good for others.

Don't expect nothing to be given to you on a silver platter, and expect everything to be taken away from you. This shows you're priceless.

Sympathy is considered weak. But being sympathetic is only possible with understanding.

Reasoning, will not only get us over the line, it will eventually remove any line of ever having to exist.

With time and patience, all will level out. As we are a part of nature, we cannot avoid its laws.

In reality, if we did not create currency in order to do business. Then all other forms of trade or bartering, would make corruption thrive.

There would be no worth, to any precious stone or metals, if it wasn't for our existence.

Groundbreaking discoveries are usually those that are sponsored and invested by breaking the ground. Ironic.

It's reasonable to say that we are all different. But it is not reasonable if we all live so differently.

Only through flexibility can we all live together. But only through a concrete and United approach, can we save the planet we all live on.

Do not always approach a situation with a planned attack in mind. For in truth, you can never foresee the planned defence you are to attack.

The same rainfall will bring life to one field, and flood the other. Positivity and negativity really depends on how and where you see it.

There is and always will be justice. But as we have chosen the life we have created, it's not wise for us to determine what justice will be.

Help. When you can. Help. Where you can. Help. What you can. But do not say, you are helping, if you're destroying or ruining.

When you take, you must give. When you give, you must not expect. But when you abuse, expect, for much to be taken, without a reason.

Do not feel obliged to fulfil a promise. There is a difference between fulfilling a promise where you are respected, and where you are used.

Everyone will blame money as the root of all evil, whilst at the same time, everyone doing all evil, is to gain that money.

The time we spend focusing on bringing down anything that is good, is a reflection of how good most of us really are.

It is inescapable. We have always been the problem, yet, the most amazing thing is, we are the only ones who can also be the solution.

A PC will process all the information within its grasp, to come to the correct answer. So too must we all.

I came to realise, there is neither a beginning nor an end. But, it is simply existence. The less the majority try to understand its completeness, the better it is for all.

The sounds of music, will not always bring you joy and happiness, but it will always bring out your emotions.

It is easier to understand the thinking of one nation, then it is to understand the thoughts of one person. Only because, each nation relies upon a few people, to raise it up.

When you approach someone who is smiling, they aren't always happy, and those that aren't smiling, may be thinking up a way to make others happy.

It is not easy for anyone. Who ever makes such a statement, that it is, Is yet to understand the full realities of this life.

It is tricky if you learn too much. It is difficult if you know too little. But it is easy, and effortless, if you show neither. Strength is knowing how to show it.

The same guardians will bear many different names, depending on culture and belief. But for them, we have always been one and the same.

A message that is intended for all, will be understood and received only by a few, and those intended for a few, are usually adopted by all.

The operator you see in movies, is not the same way the operator works in reality, and the operators themselves, are not all the same.

The foundation, is not strongest because of the material used. But, how it is planned and designed, before it is formed.

When you cannot see because of the darkness, do not feel afraid. Remember, that you can always find what is most bright, within yourself.

We have all hurt, and we have all cried. But not all of us hurt, when somebody else cries.

The same statement will be interpreted in so many ways, that at times, there is no way forward, except, by giving up on explaining.

Not every action can be understood, not because we don't see it for what it is, but because we are told, what it is not.

Double standards are only the norm, when we allow what is not normal.

Some people choose their past, and others have it placed upon them. Some people choose their future, and others have it chosen for them. Few fight so both become true and free.

The shadow is there, not to follow your every move, but to remind you, that there is always light in this world.

Never be disappointed in disappointment. Never disappoint those who are disappointed. That way nothing will actually stay disappointing.

Sometimes opening your wings will slow you down. Other times, moving slowly, will show you when the time is right to open your wings.

Believing is easy. Trusting is hard. Sometimes we lose belief in trust though, and don't trust what we think we believe in. So remember to But if it's their, it is always accessible But if it's their, it is always accessible, waits for everyone.

The actions of few, will fuel those of many. The actions of many, will be the fuel for all.

Once there were few people, teaching through wise words. Today many know these wise words. So now, seek those who teach wisdom.

Never fall for the idea of standardisation. Nothing with such a stance has progressed, except for lesser standards.

As we progress through the evolution of technology, me must not forget, to continually apply old and forgotten, teachings and philosophy.

A step in the wrong direction will still get you to your destination. But a step in the right direction, can help many others reach theirs.

Do not be bound by the notion of gravity. For your thoughts are free from its influence.

Do not learn everything about one thing, you may become limited. Learn a bit about everything, you then, have the potential to become limitless.

We were never designed to be equal in a honorary status. But we were always given the chance to view each other equally.

Not everyone was born with the chance to be able to become a genius, but everyone born, possessed the chance of becoming a genius.

When we complicate what is simple, we learn nothing. But when we learn to simplify what is complicated, we learn everything.

Through words, we write laws, we teach, we learn, we bring down the laws.

We tend to read words based on our feelings and experiences. But the world would be a different place if we based it upon what it is saying.

Do not always attack that which sits at the top. Most changes must take place from the bottom.

It may take one to think up a revolution. But it takes many for it to become a revolution.

Life is a simple equation. Do not return to that which feeds you, and you shall not have returned.

A good leader, requires their followers not to bow down, but only to show love, for a good leader, follows their followers.

We have cherished what we cannot reach, cheered what we cannot touch, jeered what we always see, and almost destroyed that which we all stand on.

We always refer to our problems as 'they'. No matter who it may be in the pyramid. But the reality is. 'We' have always been the problem.

Progress is always achieved within ones mind, much more than in ones life, and only few minds, have witnessed the equal achievement in life.

At times, no matter how powerful our will is to affect the elements. The ones we rely upon to show a heart, never seems to be elementary.

Can't live with it, but can't live without it. Necessary to save lives, but cause of many deaths. Always leaning, but rarely balance, yet some how balancing. Politics.

It is not important to reach out to one section of society to have a complete following. But reach out to all, with complete understanding.

There is no book or manual that will explain how anything supernatural is possible. But yet we have books that speak of such phenomenon.

There is a fine line between reality and an illusion. As there is a fine line between a dream and a dreamer.

We cannot as a society, teach children religious stories, or scientific possibilities, and then declare them unstable.

To raise a child, that learns and knows, that which others do not, is a successful life.

We'll encounter strange phenomenon in this world. If it was meant to be, do not be scared. Embrace it, no longer as strange, but as natural.

Most of our life, money is required for all our happenings. But remember, the rain falls freely, and the air does not cost a dime.

Do not view the negatives as a downward point in life. Do not choose to see them from an emotional point of view. View them educationally.

Destiny and destination. In reality we all move towards the same destination, but live a delusion in its approach towards its destiny.

If so many different creatures were placed on the same planet, then it was with a purpose. By removing their purpose, we remove reality.

Words and thoughts never are identical. For it is the author, that best explains their own thoughts, whilst simultaneously, using words.

We tend to fear what we don't understand now. But relish and celebrate the same deeds of past individuals through stories, myths & legends.

It is always easier to blame one individual for what is not their fault, then to blame the entire world. This is not constructive education.

If the entire world was pathologically and compulsively lying to one person, and that person said a few lies. Who is considered at fault.

No one walks with a mirror in front of them through life. So in reality, no one is reflecting themselves back, no matter where or what they look at.

Do not try and explain your thoughts, if your feelings were in the right place.

The principle of a pyramid will never change. There can only be one who stands at the top, and the top always designs its foundation. But it's the foundation itself, which has the right to place upon it, its own colours.

Trying hard to be good, is only done by those who are not. So do not try harder if you are, it is good enough to be yourself.

The reality is truly great, and the possibilities are truly greater. Just because we don't speak of or admit it, doesn't mean it isn't so.

Emotions are a fact. But we cannot prove their inner existence. Some people smile when they are sad. Some will laugh when they are mad.

Never approach a situation with your heart on your sleeve. Rather, let your heart, determine the situation on approach and when you leave.

It is better to be alone and love everything, than to be with everything and love a few. But it is greatest to love everything all the time.

Do not do what you must, if it is not what must be done. But do what you must not, if it must be done.

No matter how great your intentions may be towards another. Sometimes you have to simply remember. Intentions cannot always be seen.

The clouds will forever be forming and the wind for ever be moving. But the powers at hand, will not always be showing.

Some people wish to reach out to many in order to help, and some to a few. We should never judge this on numbers, but always on intention.

There will always come a point in life, where we must weigh up the positives and negatives. When you do, let them be yours, and not others.

Sacrifice is a necessity in order to find a compatible position in life. But do not sacrifice a good life, for an incompatible position.

We cannot expect perfection from another. Nor should we try to perfect, that which has lived in an imperfect world.

We fear that which we do not understand. We attack that which seeks peace. We fight for what is not ours. But give up, for what is our right. Change.

The lives of some are simple and basic, allowing for them to be free. For others, it is the opposite, but they seek simplicity to feel free.

We will make people happy, sad and angry throughout life. We just need to learn which ones deserve these feelings, and not make mistakes.

We all reach a crossroads. It's purpose is not to choose one direction, but choose the road that teaches you of all paths. That is wisdom.

Life was meant to be easy. We've made it hard. There is a difference between having challenges to live, and facing battles to survive.

More can be said in less than 140 characters. Because, it allows for intent to be compressed, and messages to be sharp, and action taken.

Love seems dark, hate seems bright. Care is lacking, and out of sight. Return the wings, and set to flight. Return to truth, we possess the light.

If we continue to deny that which is unexplainable for now, we restrict growth. But if we acknowledge that which we see, then we advance.

The laws and realities on earth would be rewritten. I suppose, that is why it is easier to deny some truths, than change everyone's reality.

Those things we all see, but do not pronounce as truth. Will one day haunt us.

We live in a world that is governed by the need to provide facts and evidence. Even though some things are so evident, not everyone understands this as a fact.

We at times have to explain our thoughts, words and actions. But in few instances, the explanation will come from beyond the understanding of many.

In life, there is not one who will not face a life or death situation. But only a few will learn the lessons of life after such a situation.

There is no law that doesn't allow for anything to make a sudden change in direction. But some sudden changes have catastrophic consequences. Knowing them, is important.

We can all witness a miracle performed by another. But they who perform miracles, will not see the thoughts of all those who witness.

We have a tendency to leave those in charge that speak the best, and not those, who think the best. But what of those who do both.

In one way, it is good that faith teaches us of the good and bad. But in reality, by knowing of the bad, it allows for its further creation, and for its demise.

An animal is no different to a man. Bring them up with love and care, they love you back. Place them as wild, and they become beasts.

Inside us all, we are aware of something more. But through the life we've formed, it's easier to deny what's not in store.

The designs and plans, of those that were different are always rejected initially. But when there is no other way, it becomes a masterpiece.

We can be restricted by what we say, because of the legal world we live in. But if it's said intelligently, then all things can be said.

From the smallest life form, to the largest. If it is born, if it grows. It is always connected, to a mysterious world, that never slows.

The beginning will never be repeated. The journey will always be different. The end will never be the same.

It is not right to blame a person for there choice of belief. But it is less right, if a belief, does not allow for a person to choose.

There are collective challenges we seem to all understand. But then there are Individual battles, that will never be understood by the rest.

Sacrificing everything does not always take the same dimension for everyone. Everything for one, can be the heart, for another, their wealth.

We will not always understand the time and place of why things occur. But be wise, and use these moments to reflect on other similar moments.

Bow down to that which is good and honest. Bow down to that which loves and respects. But do not, bow down for the simple sake of doing so.

Our will, will one day change reality. But our will, how ever strong, will not always be able to win the hearts and minds of those resisting.

A good intention is sometimes misinterpreted based on experience. But other times, it is intentionally abused, so that you feel guilt.

Too little understanding will not allow you to move forward, but too much understanding can place you too far back. Balance understanding.

It can be in the most awkward of moments that a revelation can appear, and the most well prepared, that will make importance disappear.

What isn't but can be, everything and anything.

Trust is not something that grows, but something that is earned.

If life was just like a box of chocolates, then we are rarely offered the assorted choice. This can only change by us changing.

How can you dismiss the creator by not seeing him, when you believe in a future you have not yet seen.

Life is a struggle for everyone in their own way, but a solution exists for all struggles.

Ideas are not easy to come by, that is why you have few inventors and many builders. Yet, without either, there is no progress.

If it is choices we complain that we don't have, then start making choices to bring the chance of new choices.

It is not a matter of the rich and the poor, it is a matter of the will and the lack of it.

If the entire world had food and water, then removal of famine would eradicate thousands of other problems.

It is not about writing a quote so it sounds good, it is about the good that a quote can bring to many.

I have the will to change the world for the better, but do you have the will to endure the journey with me.

Sometimes life can make one sad, but in every sadness their is a moment of understanding. If we learn from the understanding, we learn how to be happy.

It is not quite enough to simply love someone, sometimes you literally have to be willing to die for that love, so that it lives on.

To believe is to have faith, but to have faith is to never stop believing.

For without meaning, life is worthless, and creation gives meaning to life.

Life is beautiful, but without people it is empty and void. To full fill life as intended, we must fill life with beauty.

Sometimes it is hard to be positive, but even through negativity we can learn how to fix the mistakes.

It doesn't matter whether man has been to the moon, what matters is that we keep aiming for the stars.

Philosophy is not something that should be taken lightly, rather it is something that should flow freely.

If we could understand computers to its ultimate potential, we could understand creation in its most simplest of ways.

The mind is a sense, few dare to heighten.

What would the world be without an ant cleaning up the mess left behind? So all life matters, you just have to understand its purpose.

To sacrifice yourself for a great cause, is the same as investing in a profitable business.

Hope is only lost, when you stop believing.

Faith is only real when one loves life itself, and not losing faith in life.

Respect cannot be earned, respect is something that one must show towards everyone.

To fly free like a bird, is like speaking from your heart.

Love conquers hate they say, but how do you stop hate, if love is conquered.

If you view the world as one large electrical current, then you become aware that power is limitless.

Knowledge is not always something you learn from a paper, but something that is acquired through understanding ones surroundings.

As a tree grows and spreads it branches, so too can one spread their wings and fly away like the leaves.

Without rain the grass cannot grow, nor without the sun can it rise. Therefore, without the opposite effects, humanity cannot move forward.

It is easy to learn from the mistakes of others, but it is harder for others to accept their own mistakes.

Truth can be a simple delusion, one that only exists at times when the majority says something is that never was.

Reality is a blurry line at times, for what is the reality, if we always dream of a new future.

If you view the world in its most simplest of forms, one can understand the most complex of things.

Generating power is not about what we use to create it, but how we use it.

Water is the essence of life, and so is the air we breath, through common understanding. But it is the tolerance and respect we have for one another, that is most essential in life.

A prophet/prophetess is not sent to destroy people, but to warn people of destruction. Without the warning, how can it be prevented.

To commit unnecessary murder, is to take your own life. To save one life, is to save the life of many.

There can be no afterlife, without the present one. Nor could there have been the present life, without one before.

To be humble, is to be rich at heart. To be rich only, is to be poor at heart.

It is not always a matter of choice in life at times, but the reaction is always a choice.

It is better to sacrifice oneself for something smart, than for something stupid.

Some believe in primates', being an ancestor. Others believe in their creation. Both contradict why anyone would place harm upon any life.

The chance to pick a side on a coin is 50% for the average individual, but it is a 100% chance to move forward if we all contribute.

For a beast to lose its horns, is like a human losing their hands.

For a bird to lose its wings, is like a human losing their voice.

A branch can grow in any direction, yet it is always beautiful. So why do people not learn the same principle.

To workout a mathematical problem, is nothing like finding a life saving solution.

Without science we become void, but without love, we become empty.

Family is not limited to those you're born around, but extended by those your heart feels for.

Life can appear as dark as the outside of a Raven, but as insightful as its ability to see through all life.

A crocodile may appear dangerous and viscous, but without its presence there can be no order. Same is true for humans, appearing dangerous and vicious, but without their presence, there cannot be order.

As the wind can reach out into all directions, so too must we expand our abilities to reach out in all directions.

It is not the fact that some plants are poison, it is the point of learning to use them all for the better, and not for the worse.

As tea is diluted into water and used in medicinal use, so too humans must learn to dilute themselves into the earth through understanding, and become its healing property.

The sun may be hot and dangerous, but without it there would be no water.

Not all emergency personal will be able to save lives, and not all soldiers will take lives.

The shapes of clouds are ever changing, yet the rain always falls downwards.

Sometimes it doesn't matter what you think, what matters is how you act upon it.

Life can bring the worst out of someone, but the best answers are sometimes found in such moments.

Magic is real, just look at how we breath what we can't see.

Mans greatest challenge is not himself, but the other millions of species he has to manage himself around.

Today we may fall, but tomorrow we rise. Today we may crumble because of our weak foundations, but tomorrow we can rebuild our foundations so that they can never crumble again.

Music can be the greatest retreat for billions, not because it sings to us, but because it speaks to us.

Acting is one of two things, those that use it to amuse others as a retreat from the hardships of life, and those that use it to abuse others, and try make them retreat from life.

A quote can be one of many things, but if it brings down just one person, it should not be worthy of quoting.

Life is too short, if you live it to its fullest. Yet, fulfilled, if lived to understand it.

Some believe in a greater force, and some do not. But what we all have in common is that we live side by side.

To listen to a beat is like listening to a frog croak. It can be annoying at first, unless you listen long enough to make sense of it.

To dream is not just to wish upon something beautiful, but to plan what no one else can.

Time and space can be seen as an empty place, but also as a vacuum waiting to be filled with what isn't, but can be.

It is easy to create, but it is much harder to be creative. It is easy to invent, but it is much harder to have others use your invention.

There are many stories, but there is always only one truth.

The reality is always blurred by facts, but there can only be one reality, usually unaccepted.

Life can sometimes be like a car, you don't always get where you want sooner, by pressing the gas harder.

Solutions are at times the problems, if they don't include all irrelevant factors.

It is one thing to publish a book, but another thing for your words to be heard.

The end can only mean a new beginning, and the beginning can only mean a new end. A cycle that will never stop.

We are all prophets in way or another, but not all learn to profit from each other.

Advice can be detrimental to ones success, but it can also be the demise of ones journey.

Remember to always love with a clean heart, and not to love what is not clean.

A good man will save himself, a great man will save himself, but a selfless man will save the world.

A journey can be long if done properly, and short if not considered.

Life is full of obstacles, but obstacles can be overcome.

Life does not have a manual for anyone, but by the end you can draw one up for the next person.

Some teachers learn, and some students teach.

Freedom of religion is important, but freedom is more important.

What is magic, but the introduction of ones full potential.

The brain is the most complex feature in the universe, but what then of a planet with a trillion brains.

Perfection exists. You just need to sit down, close your eyes, and breath.

It is not the cigarette that kills, but the unwillingness to fight its chemical effects.

Gravity is one of the greatest things we have, always pulling us towards our goal.

Injustice can at times feel like it lasts forever, but feeling, and reality of forever, are nothing alike.

Home is not always where you live or where you grew up, sometimes it's simply where you are made to feel worthy.

A colour does not matter, what matters is how you where it.

Disrespect is something that many become angry over, but not many of those understand why they were disrespected.

The clothes you were should never determine how you treat people or how you are treated.

A body can turn into ash, but it's remnants are still ever present within the same existence.

A heart can become hurt through being wronged, but the mind can overcome this by reacting with courage.

Sometimes power is abused by man, but with every abuse, there are consequences.

Sometimes you have to be thankful to those you can't see, and not always angry at those you can see.

Jealousy can create many problems for humanity, but understanding can be its downfall.

It is not what you eat, but how it is made.

Sometimes life can be like a burger, you don't necessarily always know what is inside.

A restaurant caters for its customers, but the food does not make itself.

Living life can sometimes be like making a burger, you can throw anything into it, but you don't always know how it will taste.

Some systems are made to fail, only because a better version was always meant to be.

It is better to fail with a beta, than with the final product.

The heights we set for ourselves, can always be conquered. But the limits that are set within the universe, are not always ours to reach for.

Life can be like the exit seat in a plane, you have a little bit more room, but the ride is the same. So make the most of your space.

Weather is a system created for life to flow, but without life as people know it, there would still be weather.

If we reach for our target bit by bit, no matter how long it takes, we always set a greater target. Progress.

A child is the most important part of life. For who else does the knowledge we leave behind go to.

If humanity has learned to forget the mistakes, then they can learn to make the most out of negatives.

To save a life is like winning the lotto, but to save many, is like winning it over and over again.

A saint does not ask to be rewarded for a miracle, and existence does not ask to be payed for a gift.

Truth is what determines the future of life after this one, and lies are what takes you to where you thought never existed.

Money doesn't always determine ones happiness, but happiness can be taken away through money.

To help through money can be a good deed, but to ask for it back can be a wrong doing. But to ask for money, in order to place another in an uncomfortable position, is an evil deed.

A good deed sometimes never goes unpunished, but a bad deed always becomes punishable.

Life is a joke for some. But for others, it's the joke they wish to remove.

A good heart can be the downfall of many, but the redemption for all.

One may not believe in the creator, but what is as important, is to believe in love.

A conspiracy can only be something for the evil of man, for when one conspires to do good, they only seek justice.

The century that man lives in, does not determine how much good or evil he can do.

The life of one, can mean the destiny of many.

Life can be like an apple, the first bite is sweet, only to become more and more sour.

Life can be like an apple, the first bite is sour, only to become more and more sweet.

There's a bond that can't be broken, unfortunately it's not spoken. But can be heard from where you stand, in the open ocean and to the sand.

To love a woman can sometimes hurt, but to keep your love secret can hurt forever.

Love can be like a roller coaster, you get moments of joy, and moments where you simply feel sick.

A woman must not serve a man, and a man must respect a woman.

Coffee may awaken the body, but the clear mind will awaken the soul.

If we all fought for greater energy, then our own expenditure would be minimised.

Finding love can be the hard part of life, but to live without it can be a lot harder.

Ideas do not grow on trees, nor do plans build themselves.

Work can be as important as not working. Understanding the difference, is the difficult part.

Sometimes doing more can be accomplished by doing less.

It is our own desire to become successful, but success is determined by happiness.

Living life to its fullest, can be a dangerous way to live, without understanding.

The spirit will be judged upon completion of the task that is set in front of one, but the body cannot be judged if it joins the spirit on its journey, and strays from evil.

Happiness is determined by ones strength, and weakness by ones sadness.

Disappointment is a part of life, but it is also a part of sacrifice.

Happiness and sadness are sometimes the same, to reach one you pass through the other.

How does one enjoy life, if they don't accept sacrifices.

To teach one how to tackle a challenge, you must understand its problems.

Ideas can be stolen, but if the ideas spread, then it has become a success, and the source is a success.

One may not be acknowledged for their achievements, but with time all become aware of those achievements.

It is at times sad to feel unacknowledged, but it is happiness to see more and more people smile.

It is better to die for the world, than for the world to die for you.

Others may read all that one writes, but they never know what is yet to be written.

Love has the potential to bring the worst out of one at times, but hate will bring upon even worse.

Life can be like a candle, the light can always be reignited after it goes out.

The sweetness of a chocolate, can bring out the sourness of a toothache.

If life could be controlled with a remote, then you would be limited with your directions. That is why freedom is worth fighting for.

The body can feel like it's under ice, but the heart can burn bright to melt through.

It is neither a glass half full nor half empty, it is a glass always full of something.

A fish only dies out of the bowl if there is no water surrounding it.

Intelligence is not always something you're born with, but something you can learn by the actions of others.

Perfection may not exist with minimal understanding, but from afar, perfection is real.

Death may be the end of the body, but life does not end.

Watching the TV is like speaking to others, you are not always heard, but you are part of the conversation always.

A breath of fresh air can revive the lungs, and also experience life.

Wisdom is not something that grows on trees, nor is it something that falls from branches.

Reality is only what the majority understand, delusions are what the minority knows to exist.

Telepathy is exactly like a mobile phone, you need to make the call to be heard.

A true Saint is one who sacrifices themselves for the sake of many others.

Having a break is not about what you do, but what you don't do.

Writing rhymes is meant to catch the attention of the audience, to make you think and tickle your conscience.

If it were love that was to be conquered, then it was hate that has always occurred.

To drown in your own misery, is not allowing love to feel your lungs.

We don't always decide where we are born, but we always have a choice to change our birth right.

Catching a flu can be cured, but falling in love never can be.

A saying has to reach out to all, and lift up those that fall.

Sometimes we use a pen to save our lives, but sometimes they're sharper than knives.

Music can cure a heart of its pain, but it can't always take away the stain.

We write so others read, but do we always know what we breed.

Falling in love can be the most beautiful thing, even though not all can afford that expensive ring.

A picture can tell a thousand words, but a sentence can tell a thousand pictures.

Lies are all around us, we just need to extract the truth.

The truth can be blurry, but lies are always simple.

Endings can be the hardest part for some, but for others it is a new beginning.

To behold or know of something great, is not the same, as understanding greatness beheld or knowing of.

We can't hide from people, but we seem to hide our truest thoughts from ourselves.

Energy and intentions, a mind and perception. Meanings and laws, pawns and flaws. Interpretation is one, truth when it's done.

If 100% of the greatest minds power was used, then the world would not change, just become organised.

It is not about changing the world, it's about organising the world so that the problems don't interrupt society.

In life there is the perception that sudden change is hard, but at the same time, we went from candles to light bulbs without a problem.

Simplicity may be a virtue, but complexity can be the salvation, it just needs to be understood.

It is not easily understood by all, but few have always lived, so no one surrounding them has had to fall.

Perfection can be found in humanity, but not in all individuals, rather it is found in the collectiveness of the species. One just has to put the puzzle together.

We seek salvation, but why does it seem that we drive towards destruction.

Sometimes, the journey itself, is the support through life.

Saving one person, can be the start of saving everyone.

What does it mean to save, but to help all find peace from within.

It is better to sacrifice one self, than to sacrifice many.

There is no difference, in avoiding to blame the wrong person at the right time, and put blame on the right person at the wrong time.

Without a tree, we have no perception of reaching out. Save the tree, and you save yourself.

Every action does not always have an equal and opposite reaction. Bane's theory.

The economy cannot grow, if business does not reach out.

We are all different, yet we all breath the air.

An organisation cannot earn respect, if it does not allow for discounts.

Love can hurt more than pain, because it can leave both a temporary and permanent pain.

You cannot know what falling in love is, until you experience it.

What is pain, but the simple fact of your soul suffering.

All were children once. All cried. There is no one who did no shed a tear on earth. Everyone has therefore experienced love and pain.

Music can be the magical touch found only on earth, a noise we here from our very own birth.

Disasters can happen on a daily Occasion, but it's our courage that takes us to the next station.

Sometimes we misjudge the actions of others, like the misunderstanding between two brothers.

We don't always make the right choices, nor do we always listen to the right voices.

Surrounding your self with positivity isn't always possible, but surrounding yourself with too much negativity, you're responsible.

A poetic quote can help to heal the world, it's like straightening out what is unnaturally curled.

It is easier to write a rhyme that makes no sense, then to sell a quote for a couple of pence.

Sometimes it is not what you say, but how you use the words to play.

Life can be difficult up to the point of no surrender, but if you choose wisely, a chance can be offered at the right vendor.

Choices can be a difficult decision, but more dangerous is a thoughtless collision.

Gratitude for ones thoughts and feelings can go without acknowledgement, but the more it persists, the more recognisable it becomes.

Sometimes I forget the life of One as if it never occurred, but because of his suffering the whole of society has been stirred.

David was once a man to be reckoned with, but it was he, who was his own Goliath.

Moses parted the sea with the power of the almighty, so was left a sign, that not all men are to be taken lightly.

If you are not woken at the time you see most fit, sometimes it takes help from others for the light to be relit.

Power was never created to be abused, but carefully was it always to be used.

Love and anger can be the fuel of glory, or they can be the destruction if considered poorly.

Religion is unfortunately viewed by many as a setback for society, but there has always only been one truth, around which all is based.

We don't always have to believe that there is a creator above, but it is always important to remember that when we are born, we were filled with tears and love.

Sometimes mistakes are made because of the thoughts and actions of others, but it is always important to remember, to keep love for all forgotten sisters and brothers.

It isn't always easy living in a world filled with so much confusion, but in the end there is always retribution.

Hate and anger can cause the problems of the world we live in, but understanding and cooperation can overthrow this and defeat the problems.

Live not to lie.

We are all born for individual roles in the lives of others, some have one role model and others have many teachers.

Depression can be the cause of so much pain for many, but anyone can overcome this by rising up steady.

What is failure, but the inability to get back up and try again.

Progression cannot be without mishaps.

The end is never what it seems, nor is the beginning the only time the light beams.

Disappointment can occur in every day life, but revival can always be found after a little strife.

It is not always how we wish for it to be, but in the end it is always the same, all eventually see.

Sometimes life throws at us its greatest challenges, other times it gives us it's best reassurances.

Doesn't matter how good a teacher may be, if the student does not tune into what is being taught. But a good student, will learn to question everything.

We choose what we wish to do at times, other moments it comes down to another's rhymes.

Ideas can be stolen and taken from the original source, but for such a mind there is no need for a real course.

It is important to wish to help many in need, that way you defeat those full of greed.

There are times when your voice may not be heard, but then there is the moment your message is spread by that little bird.

Language can be a barrier for many in the world, but your thoughts and feelings are universal for the wider world.

The universe is a place of great love and disappointment, but it's also worth the sacrifice and investment.

Not all may be able to see that far into the future, but without commitment there is no new path.

To have the will to change what does not work, can only be accomplished through dedication.

Moments come across a soul in which it has no more will, but if you never give up, you will always find an unknown skill.

Forgiveness can be the hardest point in life, but by moving forward, it is easier to accept all that was not right.

Sacrifice is like lending your soul until you reach the finish line.

Not everyone believes in the creator, but for some he is truly the salvation for many. This belief by many, in itself creates an ever lasting creator, that can never be defeated.

A flower can blossom in the right months, but grass will always grow.

Evil only exists if you allow it.

Marriage does not matter by whom it is conducted, but only by the two giving their oath for life.

Sometimes we are surrounded by what appears to be no choice, but Someone will always hear your voice.

We all have a guardian in life, some are in the flesh, and some are in the spirit.

Subdivided destiny, is remembering right information, recognising education, and understanding what one can see.

A song does not have to rhyme to reach out to an audience, because a few good words can always tickle your conscience.

The light will always shine, neither can the flame ever go out.

Secrets do not exist, it's just that a few know of the truth.

The truth always comes to light, even though at times it seems to be no where in sight.

I will show now, and, live till all see.

Don't ever give up if someone else has done you evil, just keep your head up and don't ever let it bring you ill.

Staying strong can be the hardest thing if you've been hard done by, so just keep moving forward and sometimes don't be shy to cry.

It can be the most difficult of times that a mastermind is awoken.

They may be stealing thoughts, using ideas, taking words, but, they still come from the source.

The media can be your worst nightmare, or it can be your best friend. As all things, it must be used wisely.

If one man changes the world, it can only be for the better.

Never fall down after a failed attempt, it is only one more try till you reach the end.

To lose gracefully is the same as standing up after you trip over.

They may trick you and laugh, but remember who you are and keep moving forward.

It may get confusing through rough days, but just keep playing the right plays.

We may become disappointed with what we are given, but as long as we return more, no one can ever take it all.

Perhaps the greatest gift is health, and perhaps the greatest curse is wealth.

It is one thing to be rich in your heart, and another to be wealthy from the start.

Wealth does not determine who you will become, it is a choice within your choices.

It is easy to complicate a simple matter, but it's hard to simplify a complex one.

We all have a spark of genius in our minds, but what it's used for determines its worthiness.

If there were two of everyone, by the next generation there would be none.

Looking into the future is a gift few have, but to use it, can have consequences.

A man should not be like a rabbit, where they just look to eat and run away as quick as possible.

It isn't aliens that would be the problem, it's the way we live on earth.

When your mind goes blank, it is the doings of another. In this instance, reclaim your space.

Life is sometimes like looking at the ocean from above, it's full of life, you just need to go in to search for it.

Destiny will take us through thick and thin, but in the end we all have a chance to take control of it.

We may be made to look like fools in one time or another, but just remember, those are the moments that teach you most about life.

When you have nothing to lose, and your life is being pulled apart, to do what is honourable, is what makes heroes come true.

If it was life that was granted for it to be lived joyfully, then that is what all must fight for.

It's easy to be positive, just remember that all is living.

Not everyone lives, not everyone suffers, not everyone starves. But everyone breathes. Everyone experiences the same life.

Negativity can fuel the most positive ideas, and positivity can fuel the most negative responses. So always be positive, but neither is it good never to see what is negative.

If you have to fight for something, ask yourself if there is only one winner.

We are all born to eat and drink, but not all of us know how to think.

Prejudice, always claimed not to exist, collectively. But it has never been more visible than today. If continually accompanied with a lack of knowledge, freedom can become lost.

Information learned, is never restricted to one form. More importantly, critical thinking itself, is perhaps the best new information source.

It is better to be in the public eye and suffer, than to rejoice alone. It shows you the true nature of what surrounds all.

A bird can be a blessing in disguise for a person, yet a person seeks two knock out two birds with one stone two many times.

A barking dog is more dangerous, because it speaks to you.

Love for life is generally rewarded only in the end.

The evil doings of another can bring the greatest injustice towards a man, but the strength of the man can bring the greatest justice to many others without him even being aware.

How do you rejoice when your life seems to be the life of the world, and the world fails to hide its life from you.

How does one believe in humanity, when the greatest lies are by humanity. Only by remaining humane.

One will concentrate with maximum effort to bring forth ideas for the world, and yet it only takes minimal effort for the world to return the favour.

Don't expect to be rewarded for the hard work of others, but only for your own.

Thoughts are powerful, but will is stronger.

One can be cheated on, one can cheat, but in the end all only hurt themselves.

How can a dream not be taken seriously, when the imagery is based on our lives!

Things don't just cross someones mind. Ideas, plans, thoughts, experiences and reasoning. This and much more, is brought forward by all the information one has accumulated.

More can be done at times by not moving than by moving. The purpose is understanding movement.

Never generalise. One is allowed to believe in the creator, and yet still love all sciences, philosophies, engineering, architecture, history, and apply criticism to all.

Not right to blame those that don't understand. They know, no better. But neither should one who understands be blamed, by those who know, no better.

Train your mind, to remember everything that's heard. Not so that it is maliciously used. Because what you hear now, may seem out of context, but at a later date, it may make more sense.

Law is the basis of all existence. Known and practiced in many forms. But when, ones ability exceeds known or accepted law, than miracles can occur more visibly.

No one can hide, but no one should ever have to run.

When powerful, learn to be humble, when strong, learn to be noble, when wise, still seek wisdom, when good, spread that nature, and life can change positively.

Law was not designed, for attacking. Law was designed for defending.

There are many forms of communication. But above them all and for them all, the one required always, and most powerful, is language of words, because it is understood and spoken by the majority.

Searching for the unknown, without connecting with the known, is only possible to be understood, if both the known and unknown are understood.

When one is given very little in life, their gifts are a way of healing.

To make another smile, can be the greatest gift.

To help those in need, does not only come through a drink and a feed.

Lioness locked, but heart still free, respects power, man can't see. Calmly lays, enjoys the presence, knowing inside, same feeling in essence.

Reincarnation is the reality of many but not of all.

A blessing will come as a disguise, but a disguise can also haunt you forever.

You cannot clone the original source. For originality cannot be destroyed.

The truth has always prevailed, sometimes it comes over night and other times a thousand years later.

Truth is always known, but it's holders do not always share it.

Binding all natural elements is a gift only given by God.

You can listen close and try to destroy a good being, but in the end the ones that suffer are those who unknowingly try to destroy the good being.

Goodness and beauty comes in all shapes and sizes. It is also not always beautiful in appearance, but then again, who determines what is beautiful in appearance.

You can try and trick one to go to hell, but when they decide to go to hell on their own, you will never understand why.

There are many places likened to hell on earth, which leads many to think, perhaps there is no hell, except the ones created by humanity.

The dolphin feels, what one is missing, love that's lost, emotions kissing. Connects inside, a way unspoken, some with nature, remain unbroken.

One can be both spiritual and materialistic. For is it not a good spirit that creates a device that is used for good by the people.

Water can drown you and it can save your life.

Near every ending, all think the same!

With all words, the source is always found.

My goodness cannot be taken away from me, nor should you ever let it be taken away from you.

If you listen closely, you will hear only, what you were taught never exists.

All life speaks to us, but not all hear their cry.

It is not the rock that can speak, it is what touched the rock, that tells its story.

If you close your eyes, you will see better. If you shut your ears, you will hear better. If you switch your mind off to your surroundings, you will hear what you are surrounded by.

Jealousy comes from a place far away from here. Or is it taken from here to far places.

Once upon a time there was love, now all crave it again.

The snake does not strike to kill, it hisses to warn.

What is paranoia, but a state of extra awareness!

To be wrong about something, is to know how to approach it the next time.

To be scared for others, is a fear we should all possess.

To love another, and fear for their safety, is an emotion that children are born with.

We don't choose what will happen to us as children, but we choose how we tackle the issue.

Love is like a spec of sand in the ocean. It can dissolve into the water, and through the body of a creature. But it will always exist in one form or another.

There is a thin line between jealousy and fear, and a difference between fearing jealousy, and admitting it.

Intentional Behaviour that causes a lie towards a few, but hurts no one, seeking the truth, can always be forgiven. But a lie that hurts all, is hard to forgive.

Sometimes we tell a fib, to get to the truth.

Not all will forgive a lie, but if it reaches a greater truth, it will be forgotten.

Truth is important, but if it hurts many, a lie will sometimes be easier to bear.

It is at times easier for the people to live a lie, than to live a truth they will find hard to understand.

We are all kings and queens, but not all work for the people.

The universe is like the inside of a closed off glass, it is spacious, but you don't always know what is on the other side.

We may not always find our soul mate in this life, but when we do, we feel it.

This life and the next may not be the same. But a true friend in this life, will make the journey to the next easier.

Understanding is the most important thing in life. For without it, we are only playing a guessing game.

Our life may be a game for some, it may be tools for others, but for me, I feel it with my entire essence.

We don't necessarily choose what occurs throughout life at all times, but somewhere out there, we all have our guardian.

Some angels fly through heaven, and others are born on earth.

It wasn't creation that chose for our lives to be hard, it was collective choices that led us to having to find solutions to the problems the collective created.

Some of our problems are not created by us, and others are only solvable by us.

Life at times feels like the matrix, we sometimes feel restricted by movement, played like toys, and controlled by a machine. But if you look deep enough, an organic machine is exactly what everything is, and if a soul is born within an organic life, then it can be with a machine.

Perhaps the truth hurts for most, but for me, no matter how unbearable, it is always important to know the truth.

One can live with pain, beyond all measures. But understanding why and when they smile, is the fascinating bit.

Happiness is not always in the form of satisfaction for oneself.

What is a blessing, but the simple good deed of a fellow life form to another.

The light can never be captured. It will always be free.

Perhaps many are being fooled in the world every moment, but if many are real and true to themselves, then that is all that matters.

It's hard to believe in good, or mercy for all life forms at times, because of collective understanding, and livelihood. But isn't the simple gift of life, worthy of praise, and worth fighting for.

Even through hardships, be glad that you have been born. For it is only in life, that one can learn what the mind truly is.

Telepathy is an unspoken part of everyday life. But it is as real as the air we breath.

You cannot choose who you are born, or the gifts/talents placed upon me. But you can choose what you wish to do with it and for who you wish to use it.

Mistakes are a daily occurrence, but solutions are lacking.

The universe is like the ocean. You may travel large distances, but life is scattered everywhere. There is no device that can see what is at one end from the other, except itself.

Are we not all aliens in one way or another. Does earth not travel around the sun. Does the galaxy not travel within the universe. Bringing us into a new place in space every moment.

It is difficult to understand the Unknown for most. But it only takes a few to see what is for what it is, for most to move to the next level.

We are not a game of fun. We just do not all listen!

The universal law does not always prevail in the instance. But neither is a spec of sand touched for millennia.

Confusion can be caused by the simplest misunderstanding, and it can take the most complex explanations to unravel.

Sometimes we speak a language understood only by a few, and sometimes we need to learn quickly.

Somethings change instantly, and others change over time, but if we have good intentions, it doesn't matter how long it takes!

The energy that we do not see, is the energy that will be most profitable.

If we all thought the same, than there would never be any changes, and if we all thought differently, changes would never come to fruition.

If one was to view the earth from afar, the secrets of discovery appear so simple.

No vision of life suits all. But some visions, are worthy of being placed as foundations, to which all other visions can be placed within.

Artificial intelligence may not be the answer when it comes to complete control, but without it, there is much that cannot be accomplished, based on current development.

It will not be AI's that are the problem, it will be the programming that people apply to its creation.

Let the clouds show the pictures of the journey, the rain the tears of the pain endured, the lightning the power it's become, and the shinning stars, its everlasting light.

Perhaps we are not always heard on time, or perhaps the problem is we did not speak the right language.

All languages were created.

If the raven speaks, it does so silently, mans perception, views it violently. Sips the water, by the side, no ones alone, on the ride.

If we can dream of the stars, then everything is possible on earth.

No one who is part of the problem for someone, has the right, even by thought, to think they know what is best for that individual. Irony.

The right mind, was placed upon the right shoulders.

A message, both indirect and direct, can be both good intended, and deceiving. Only practice, teaches which one is which.

Some things are written to help everyone, and others to help someone heal.

There are so many people who wish to guide someone home, where ever that may be. But through complications of life, one cannot always tell you where that is.

Some did not write or sing all their songs, they usually just dream up the words!

The age does not matter, nor a body of old or young, but will to do good, will be ever lasting!

There is no force that can take away from one, who they are, for it is the forces, who wanted us to see for ourselves.

Respect is not a one way stream. Respect is a two way road. Streams dry up, and eventually stop flowing. Two way roads, can be continuous.

Love, brings calm, the perfect weather, for body and soul. Sudden changes, will bring forth sudden gusts of wind, and no force will stop it.

Don't always write so that it sends a message to all. Sometimes just place your own feelings, as a way to walk after you learn to crawl.

I may not succeed tomorrow, or in the way you see fit, but I'll try do as much good in this world, bit by bit.

Some emotions are powerful and thoughts are strong, but the way some express themselves in words may sometimes appear wrong.

If lies, became the norm, and truth became punishable. The future, has already been determined.

If we listen to the right person at the right time, we would be closer to perfection without committing a crime.

Law is there to protect the ones who are different and in need, and sometimes it appeared that the lawless who must lead.

When you think, think clearly and deeply, and when you read these words, think on your own, and apply it to your life.

Important if we could all be a helping hand to another, because some don't have a true sister or a brother.

The wind cannot take away your ideas or your thoughts, it can only spread it further away.

Don't be embarrassed if you are the laughing stock of a few, because if you are different, remember it's a reason to be proud of you.

Our life will take us through a journey with twists and turns, so fear not evil, for its the light of goodness that burns.

Keep it real from day to day, a good soul we must all stay, everywhere we see snakes and ladders, but goodness is all that matters.

If you find it hard through your days because of that voice, switch it off, and listen to the words it writes.

Don't be scared if you do not understand the voice you hear, slow it down, and know that in the right direction it will eventually steer.

The games being played through the technology we've created can be hurtful, that is why we need technology that will become helpful.

The mind does not go blank but the thoughts can become still, yet the heart will still burn and carry the strong will.

The mind is the energy. The energy is the mind.

There have been many great minds that have helped build this world, but in history there has always been one that has made the silent changes for all others.

It is difficult at times to reach out and have everyone understand what you think, but if it makes them think, half the job is done.

Being lost happens to everyone in one point of time or another, but remember you can always then, only be found.

There is no such thing as invisibility, if it is there.

It is easier to believe in a mind that doesn't think, than in one that thinks outside the box.

Rewards are like the leaves that fall off trees, you pick them up in Autumn, and wait for them to grow again.

The difference between an idea and a creator, is that the idea cannot be put forward properly, without the ideas of the creator.

We dream big, and stoop low, think small, and live high. I don't like that. Time to live the dream.

People are scared of the Unknown, so they ask for the need to be controlled. Because, without knowing, they fear of the unknown.

Some philosophical statements, are not only philosophical. They are also the basis of laws, both universal and earthly, theories, and inventions.

Not all can understand the thoughts of one, for when it appears negative, it can actually save many.

No one should wish to die when they are given life, and no one should wish to take life, when they did not give it.

We take for granted those that speak good words, because of those that hurt us with the same words before.

It may be a game for some with what they wish to achieve, but if they don't understand what they're doing, then show them it's not a game!

Our body does not always lie to us, nor does it always speak the truth, but the mind is one place you can bring forth positivity and understanding to it all.

It becomes difficult when you hear so many languages spoken, that it takes courage to understand what is broken.

Instinct and intuition can lead us to salvation, but not hearing right can become an abomination.

Righteousness and a good heart is what we all dream of, so trust in those two things always.

If we do not see on time what may be the issue with our own life, if you've done no evil in your heart, stay true even through strife.

We cannot always prove to our fellow humans our thoughts and what stands behind, but it is important that the meaning is what we all find.

We are in a way a matrix of some sort, connected to a universe with a limitless port.

If we only believed in what was in front of our eyes, then gravity would be greater and we would never glare up at the skies!

It is important to understand that education is of relevance to humanity, for without it, humanity would never have defied gravity.

Speed is too often measured by what is viewed by sight, forms of matter, or energy. But speed, exists in many forms, it's immeasurable.

Perhaps it is not the crafts we build that will take us far into space, but our work on the spiritual side of the human race!

Science has reached a great distance from the days of old, but we have yet to utilise that which comes from the cold.

Chemistry is the key to take us into the unknown, for is it not the main ingredient from which we are created.

The creator played his part in creation, and appeared to disappear, not because he left us, but so we can define our own lives.

It is hard at times when we feel that no one can hear us, but it can be harder when everyone can hear.

A channel of communication is usually designed through technology, but that which is not explainable, is there for a purpose.

We make mistakes we are not always aware of in life, and sometimes we are not aware others caused our mistakes.

Do not always listen to what you don't understand, but try to always understand why you don't listen.

There are so many intelligent people in the world, but rarely can they see what is truly out there.

Our restrictions upon ourselves to believe in a greater reality, is what makes us limited in our achievements.

Perhaps by writing, one can change the world for the better, but sometimes it is to simply reach out, to something they cannot teach others to understand.

It is not sacrifices by one that always leads to a new discovery, but the willingness of many, to believe in a new reality.

We must learn to recycle all materials to move forward.

With all the chaos in the universe, does one not think, how we have survived for so long.

Magic is a word we have defined to our own understanding, but in the universe its definition is one of different understanding.

The energies that surround us are not always measurable by technology, and not only through technology can we reach those energies!

The mind is of complex nature. Not because we are unable to understand the brain, but because we do not wish to accept the power of the spirit.

Speed is an Illusion we create for ourselves, because we lack the belief that was placed or created by us.

Our Gravity was placed as a playground for our beginnings, so we understand the playing field outside.

Mind over matter is a statement not yet understood. Because we use matter still, not all concentrate on the mind.

The only part of the body that makes us civilised, is our brain. But not all utilise it.

No one truly understands how it all works, for if they did, they would be the only ones necessary.

The universe was devised so that we all learn to work together. If we fail, do we start again.

Existence will always exist, but what exists within it from now on, we can decide.

We all become obsessed with our own ego, but not all of us understand it may effect others.

Good intention is of absolute importance, and listening to others can be even more so.

The universe can be considered like a mind of its own, for when something happens that no one understands, it is the only force you can reference.

We should not always dive into the unknown to learn what is not for us, and a sign for anyone, is when they keep getting burned.

Science is a language that was put together to help us move forward, but can be the demise if used improperly.

Sometimes we are unable to protect ourselves in all forms and manners, but if we stay alert, that is all that matters.

It can be confusing at times by being aware of ones surroundings, because the extra senses tell you not all is fine, but those around you try and make you feel comfortable.

Not every word is always meant to teach the world, at times it's directed at a few, in order to help them understand.

I know there is always one that stands out among the crowd, but there are also those that hide themselves, because they are not heard, but wish for others to listen.

Is knowing too much a threat, or is it not knowing enough that is a threat.

The chemistry we now understand can enhance one self, but can also minimise ones hearing capabilities.

Sometimes we must listen with our eyes, and hear with our intuition.

Technology has reached an age of evolution, not because of its advancements, but because of its connection to biological life.

It is not yet understood, what has the greater power, the spirit or technology. But without the spirit, life would be no longer.

We all see what others cannot, but it is important to remember, there is always only one truth.

We speak languages to communicate, but those that are unspoken, can be the loudest.

Sign language can be deciphered, but a language of signs is much harder.

There are interruptions in communication all around us, so if you do not hear something correctly now, go over it again later.

The planets are not yet understood for their influence, and earth is not yet understood for its powers. It is information of interpretation that causes the confusion.

Search for the right frequency, listen in the right direction, and you may always walk the wrong way.

It is hard to not recognise the anomalies, but it is harder at times to notice the obvious.

Study not what is wanted or misunderstood by the intelligence of the unwise, but to move forward, study what they are disconnected from.

It can be a crazy world, where the sane are considered insane. But it is crazier to know of your sanity, and drive yourself insane.

It has always been a world of communicative warfare, but no war can be caused from a minimal amount of information.

It is never the time to forget about the creator, but it is neither the time to forget about our progress.

If the right steps are not made within the current technological leap, no steps can be made to reverse its consequences.

"A" mind can see what others cannot perceive, but others perceive only what they understand.

It is not robotics that will create the issues of the future, but the programming that accompanies it.

It is we that must expand our own physicality with advancements, to prevent the Unknown from being in full control.

It is the part of yourself which you cannot see that will save the day, and not what you see, which can only ruin everything.

It is of necessity to save those that are different and see the truth, so that all can be protected.

If you do not understand the greater picture with which we are part of, then it is important to concentrate only on the section that you understand.

In a way everything is a mess, but then again, without a mess, you cannot tidy up.

The order of how things work has never been perfected. It will always be a work in progress, determined by the acts of individuals.

If it wasn't for music, many would suffer. If it wasn't for musicians, music would suffer.

Propaganda is so confusing. Only because it is so obvious.

Some theories stand strong, and others fail early. But it's those, that circulate for too long, without definitive conclusions, that has the ability to halt progress.

If life was a mirage, or a dream of one, then we are living in the most amazing mind in existence.

Science, even though broader than other areas of study, is only a name of an entire area of study. Not an entity, that agrees with itself, within itself.

Sweet words are the basis of love and comfort, until they are the deception of hate and discomfort.

Education is the most amazing creation in existence. Until we confront that which cannot be taught.

We must learn more about ourselves and our reason for creation. Without this we become confused, and lose focus for salvation.

We are free to be spiritual, but are our spirits free to be emotional.

The speed of light is the quickest speed humanity is able to perceive, because the body cannot understand beyond that.

If the small moon affected the earth, then the planets are playing games with us.

Long ago a man walked many miles to find his peace, today it is called meditation.

We never know how the beast will awaken, because when it was gentle we put it to sleep.

When you throw a curve ball, makes sure it doesn't have too much momentum, in case it goes back around.

I guess it is easier to lie throughout life, I mean, it becomes easier for the truth bearers.

Is it humbling to live a deceptive life. It's like drinking sea water, and saying that it is sweet.

What are we really searching for through science? Same thing as religion! Just another way of approaching it.

If you make a movie of aliens, no question is asked. If you speak of aliens, too many are asked.

The Zoo is like the Galaxy, it brings together that which never knew of each other.

Isn't it interesting that light defies gravity, yet we do not apply it to universal research.

Instant messaging. Defies all logic of scientific understanding.

Never dream small, and don't be scared of dreaming too big. Because you never know what is real beyond our understanding.

Sometimes we listen and understand the truth, but the world doesn't always respond to thoughts, but to acting.

Life throws us the most untaught challenges, we have to adapt so quickly, or be true to ourselves and suffer the consequences.

I guess we all know that everybody is lying in one form or another, but understanding why these lies are so prevalent, would take too many resources.

I guess it is easier to blame one individual when many make mistakes, as creating proof becomes much easier.

Justice is not always fair, but it is neither always understood when the complication of a situation is beyond ones understanding.

Sicknesses are claimed to be understood, but the same symptoms can be applied to both a rare illness and a simple flu.

We tend to wish we can believe those that we love, even though they prove so many times that they wish evil upon us, claiming it through love.

Fear is something that is not built into our biology, and if the mind understands this, then biology can be defeated.

We all have a certain amount of will, but not all will, can overcome matter.

If games are being played by society, then real life loses its purpose.

There are signs all over the world that are there to help, but some signs are artificial and based on opinion, while others are natural.

It's hard to fight the ones you love, because there intention is not always for the same love you feel.

Nano technology has taken great leaps in this world, but the spirit is still determined to fight its negative effects.

Chemistry is known to be able to cause unnatural effects upon the body, but it can also excel the body to the next level.

It's ironic that when a scientist or a few, make a great change, that science is given credit. But Law is not, when a lawyer brings forth great change.

Sometimes when you love too much, it is not perceived by what your heart feels, but as jealousy.

The hardest thing in life is accepting the games played upon your soul, when ones intelligence is spun inside out, causing confusion.

Unfortunately we must travel through part of life in the body, an instrument that can be manipulated if one is not careful.

Sharing thoughts through technology was a creation, one that would duplicate the natural thought sharing we did not understand.

We are born naked, but to truly being naked and not ashamed, is to never be understood.

It is not hard to be heard all the time, but it is much harder when what is heard is artificially caused.

To be in sync can scare many, but not to be in sync anymore, scares some.

A network of information flowing, without modern technology, is, and was always there.

If we listen closely to our past, and understand the present, we realise, the only things changing, is our place in spacetime.

I guess we can't change the games that are applied by people politely, in which case, one should simply disconnect.

If you are afraid, do not seek to hide from what scares you, but try to understand it.

Space and time, they are both spaceless and timeless. Because, there will always be existence!

Realistically, with all the belief systems and theories, just Keep it real, as there is only one truth.

Isn't it interesting, that even though we all look different, we can all learn the same languages, and understand the same words. Yet we are so distant!

Let's be honest, you need intelligence to create intelligence. A computer didn't evolve itself!

What if we learned to play with words, and noticed that the secrets lay in this small prevalent everyday fact.

It's fascinating that we admire the artistry and brilliance of extraordinary figures, but always apply a problem when we don't understand them.

It is not the crazies that changed the world, it's those that were never understood.

Philosophical words are great when they make sense, but what about when they contradict each other?

I guess many apply the words that suit them in the moment, and forget those that changed their lives.

Historical moments were determined by politics of the time, and our destiny of tomorrow is determined by the politics of today.

How does one stay wise in a world lacking wisdom, and how does one stay humble, when we don't respect the air we breath.

We don't know what we are being born into, but we always know what we are bringing those that are being born into!

Sustainability is a dream that we must make become true, because we have never faced such a moment, until recently.

If it wasn't for governments and leaders who understood the minds of the different, earth would be the universes dumping ground.

We don't always wish to recognise what we see, mainly because we believe we can create a different outcome.

A simple phrase not understood by many, can cause the greatest positive implications by a few.

Technology has become such a commodity in our lives, sometimes the ideas placed upon it do not recognise the rightful owner.

An invention has many times been stolen from the source it came from, and theories attributed to those who do not understand it.

Perhaps one will enlighten the world through years of their life, but one moment is all it takes to enlighten them.

We have the ability to travel at speeds we do not understand, but we do not focus on the things we cannot see.

If the beginning of the universe spread at speeds we cannot measure, then such speeds are present still.

The selectivity of information is widely confusing. Because it can be abused by the majority, and not taken into consideration when used appropriately by the minority.

I dwell on understanding many times, but then I realise, most do understand. But do not accept that they do not understand!

We can save a life in one moment, and make a mistake the next minute. But it is at times the mistake of one minute, that is only remembered.

It appears so, that asking kindly, is abused, and asking angrily, you are abused.

The earth is always rotating in the same motions, yet its momentum does not determine the impacts within it.

If nature works in mysterious ways, does it not require an intelligence that is self aware to stand behind its works!

If the creator is the father and earth is the mother, then we have not treated out parents correctly.

It is at times best to isolate yourself. Just ask the many that changed your lives, if they did it in a crowd.

How can you blame an individual and destroy their life, if all they have done is seek kindness and freedom, in order to help many.

There are many songs, shows and movies depicting life. Yet, if spoken to the wrong individual, or to the wrong individuals, it can be used against you.

It is at times, best to understand that you will never be understood, than explain, what they cannot understand.

Family and friends are most important in life, only if they respect you for who you are.

Society is not use to those that are able to do many things, so it is important then, for you to understand this principle within society.

Do not always be ashamed if you are misunderstood, rather, understand, that not all trees grow at the same rate.

Some branches reach out further than others, and some roots, never stop spreading.

One must accept the realities of life, and to propel the rest forward, one must accept the realities others are unaware of.

The creator is a touchy subject, not because we don't understand what our part is in life, but because we don't accept his place in ours.

To be accepted, one must raise a family. But it is usually those that are unable to, that help those that only know such a way of life.

Everyone can feel at one moment or another that they are not understood by the world, but to actually not be understood, that is a feeling not many have.

We create and sell comics and books depicting supernatural figures, and celebrate them. But imagine they appeared in reality!

The DJ will play your favourite track, but life will not always work in the rhythm that favours you.

Disturbances can be the most annoying factor of everyday life, but can also save you if you understand its purpose.

Do we regard ourselves as civilised, even when we conspire against those that can further advance civilisation?

We will make it, we will succeed. When we do, no one to witness it, will be a failure!

As you cannot know all the information that is sent through hardware, you will also not know all that is sent through the brain.

It is fascinating that we are forced to think of "reality", as it is the only accepted reality because of our understanding.

How were prophecies or future events seen by individuals if they were not part of a greater reality.

Signals and information have become so overlapping on our planet, that every action and reaction is naturally circulating, which is where the confusion lies.

It is not important to replicate the brain, it is only necessary to understand it from the right place.

The spirit does not seek out a super computer to show its power, it seeks a strong will, to show its goodness.

A statue of an Angel will stand guard over a place of worship, but would an Angel in the flesh be respected by the worshipers.

If we are determined to all do good, then the right signs will never be lacking.

It is not the works of all life that wishes to confuse, but rather those that know too much of confusion.

Are we reincarnated like the seed spread from another plant carrying the same information, or does our soul bring things of old into the new.

The Holy Spirit is that which is beyond reach even with all our effort in research, but it's form and glory are ever present

There are no delusional thoughts, if we teach our children of Fairy's, Santa, Angels etc. We must always tread carefully with this reality.

We teach the children of the truths unspoken as adults, because as adults those truths seem punishable by law.

We can never really get rid of the truths within existence, we can only try remove them from someones life.

Sometimes we are restricted to use a few words so that a story can be told, because the story can never tell all the words we wish to use.

If we were frozen and awoken, yet time continued to flow, new year would be another day. So make your resolution daily, we designed the calendar.

As one single planet, moving within the universe, we still do not know how to celebrate something at the same time.

Isn't it fascinating, that we do not celebrate new year on other planets, but only record the amount of earth days they revolve around the sun.

As we celebrate the first day on a calendar that we designed, we must not forget, our other designs that still haunt us. These must be resolutions.

Time is a creation that allows us to be organised, allows us to have order, allows us to feel civilised. But time does not wait for our mistakes.

Once religions were formed on the basis of those who performed the supernatural. What if those today had no religion, but simply believed?

Is it not natural to be connected to the elements of air, water and earth, when the soul consumes all through the body.

If electrical currents can travel safely through our bodies, does it not imply that we are in some form connected to our technology.

It is the misconception that we are born to simply die. If we consider the cycle of rain and crops, we would understand that life never dies.

Not all energies are visible, even when they're there. We cannot see the gravity keeping earth in the direction of the sun, but do see the energy released from the sun.

It is not the clouds that hold within it the energy of the lighting strike. It is just a tool, through which it is delivered. As the motor is used for the fuel.

If life could be defined by a few words, I would say, that existence could only be known if there is life within it. There will always be existence.

Pain and suffering was a code included in life itself. Not because it is to cause hurt, but only so we learn how not to cause such hurt.

Perhaps we give away too much information to those that misuse it, and perhaps we don't give enough to those that could use it to everyone's benefit.

One could not understand the open seas without all the earths waters, nor could one understand humanity, without all the earths people's.

Within all cultures there is a lesson to be learned. For is it not through exploration that the world is what it is today.

Unfortunately there is not one religious body that is perfect. For not all great men and woman have been born into the same religion!

The creator sent many men and woman to do his deeds on earth, but never did he place all his teachings in the mind of just one, or is it so, as to spread to others.

It's easy to create a story that suits a selected few to go for glory. But only a selected few, understand what glory actually is.

Sometimes we can't fight ideologies head on, because we care for people. Fighting this best then, is through becoming universally civilised.

We will interpret one book in a million ways. But the same star was used by all people to cross the seas!

There is only one way to curb out false teachings. To teach the truth, that we were all created equal.

As we see birds migrating without borders, so too, we should spread true peace without borders.

Sometimes it is necessary to create borders in order to keep people safe. But why do we not then keep all safe within our borders?

It's a complicated life, without exaggeration. That is only because we have become a lot smarter in greater numbers.

Once the Egyptians kept knowledge a secret. Many thought it was evil. But then, too much knowledge kept hidden, can In fact be the greater evil.

Information and knowledge must always move forward and evolve. Not dwelling on the old, but learning of the new. This brings peace.

It actually doesn't matter what the majority believe. If the minority can demonstrate a better way. We all move forward.

Do not worry if what you seek is not understood, but worry that what you seek will benefit us all.

It is difficult to watch the news and see the sadness we ourselves have created. But it is much more sad, that we don't create better news.

I guess sacrifice is a difficult reality with all the prospects the modern world offers. But when did the world not offer prospects.

We accept the seeds and crops from another continent. But it seems to be all that we accept.

Is it truly a world where we are in a state of no return, or is it the return that will place us in a Worldly state!

Karma, yin and yang, an eye for an eye. Creations laws described through different teachings. Yet one that we have absolutely challenged.

Yin and yang. A little known philosophy abused by many. Never teaching the ability of one side out growing another.

We do seem to use philosophy where it suits our needs. But love is always love. So begin to love thy neighbour.

If one day we all decided to lay down our weapons and walk through the world without a care, we would understand the potential we possess.

I don't think people absolutely understand true reincarnation. Because people don't know who decides, where and what we come back into.

Sometimes we wish to spend all our days with those we love, but with this being improbable, it is important to spend all our days with love.

The soul is the binding connection between us and what is out there.

You can measure the heart, but not the soul. You can affect the brain, but not the mind. You can play with the body, but not the will.

Everyone's battle is hard. That's why it's called a battle. But fighting a battle together, always makes it easier. Our destiny then is shared.

A war, is about what it is fought with and how it is fought. Because some fight for land, but most just fight for freedom.

With our leap in technology, our understanding of the presence, this planet should have more diverse life now, but instead the opposite may become true.

We declare ourselves intelligent, proclaim geniuses, grant awards. But why do we still go backwards with our forward leaps!

Isn't it a simple idea to desalinate sea water, nourish dry land, and create a healthy ecosystem once more.

If we applied robotics to our selves in a simple manner, we would remove countless problems we have created.

Diversification is a solution, so that both the big and small are placed in a position to move forward and not cause a domino effect.

If we are able to intercept communications between technology, then we must learn how to listen to the wind.

Anyone can tell you what the weather may look like just before it arrives, but no one can tell you how the wind suddenly changes directions.

If we realised that we would one day require our natural resources for greater feats, we would begin to apply renewable energies yesterday.

We set off on all of our explorations using the wind, and then the collective suddenly stopped utilising its power.

We do not always have to go high up to create energy. Sometimes we just need to place our effort in the right currents.

There is always a solution that will not take away the power of the pyramid. It will simply spread the foundation wider.

Laws of old cannot always be applied in times of new. But sometimes we need ways of old, to not destroy the new times.

Ideas and plans are plentiful. But we always end up relying on the plan and idea of a few, so that all others could be incorporated.

It is of irreplaceable value that we have experts in all fields in life, but it is also important to have those who understand their place.

It is not politics that is the problem. It is the politics that causes the problems.

Sometimes overloading data can be the cause of the problem. So it is important to use the right data, in order to find the correct solution.

Constructive thought is hard to be understood by all, and philosophical thinking is the reason it becomes hard to understand.

The holes in the ozone layer are repairable. It is just not profitable for one business, but wisdom says that it affects all business!

Sometimes we require financial backing to have our ideas heard, but sometimes stolen ideas allow us to share these ideas freely.

There will be a day when history will be rewritten, as always occurs. For sometimes it is our own creation that will bring forth justice to past events.

If we are a form of energy which possesses information, then imagine the information stored within the energies surrounding earth, and beyond.

There has always been evolution. But isn't it interesting that we have yet to manage to spark this evolving factor in modern apes.

We can claim that something has been designed or written before us, but you can never claim that it is understood the same.

A bird is limited by law, not by its desire to be free.

The current will pull you in, but the volume of water will remain the same.

It is as great a challenge to go around the greatest mountain, as it is to go over.

It easier to understand what does not speak at times, then that which says too much.

Somethings can not be explained, and other things should not have to be explained.

To apologise when you have done no wrong, is the same as being thankful when you have been done by wrongfully.

We must be aware of the difference between hate and anger. For one must naturally feel some anger, when they are hated.

Neither freedom nor Liberty are the most important values. For without love, there can never be true Liberty or freedom.

There must be a clear distinction between serving someone, and to being someone's slave.

Inside the most evil of beasts, the most heartless of souls, there is love and understanding. That is what must be fed, to awaken us all.

Some of us can be overwhelming. But when the cry is more important than the feeling, and there is great reason, continue to be overwhelming.

Do not fear the man with hate, for you know what to expect. Fear the man with Love, for his will has never allowed hate to take over.

Through gradual progress, all good desires can be accomplished. But only evil desires seem to be witnessed by immediate actions.

Sometimes our voice will not be heard from ourselves, but through others, who spread the word, and make the voice as loud as it can possibly be.

A voice can only be as loud as others allow it to be. No loud speaker, is powerful enough to travel the globe.

People require faith. Dismissing one way of believing, and increasing one way of thinking, the void, will be refilled by undesirable faith.

Seek what you must, so you can find what is not told. But be careful when you find what must not be told, for then others will seek you.

To take ones side because they seek love and truth, is to take ones side because you also seek the love and the truth.

Never be discouraged by injustice. Only through such paths have the greatest fights been won, and the greatest obstacles conquered.

Life will not always be able to tell your story to the world, and only you may know the truth. So only you will truly know what you deserve.

Generosity should not be measured by what you give, but purely, by how much you are able to offer.

All life forms play a part in our existence. They do not all breath, grow or eat the same way. But they are all still called life forms.

It is never really the 'people's' fault when problems occur en mass. But at the same time, it is the 'people' who allow for it to happen.

Destination has rarely been known in any form of discovery, nor could we have imagined the paths brought upon by every journey. Destination?

There are engineering feats, that stand out in both times past and times of new. Both small, and large. But we have yet witnessed the future.

Mathematics can be applied to almost everything, once it has been designed or discovered. But, it is not the solution to everything.

It is hard to justify not pursuing knowledge in all its directions. But, it is harder to justify, when the knowledge pursued leads no where.

Does it really matter, in times when our future is at stake, what the beginning was. Is the future itself not more important.

The application of belief is not only found in religion or spirituality. It is the common principle on which all unproven knowledge is based.

We apply selective information, to conclude a fact, that provides a theory. But so much less effort, could solve real life issues. Confusing it can be.

If one can tell a true story in a few words, they have found the ability, to hurt very few, but help many.

Remorse can be the underlying factor, between guilt and innocence, even when the guilt, is not yours to bear, remorse, is yours to feel.

Sometimes we gamble not so we can win monetarily, but so we can gain intellectually, through experience, and awareness of how things work.

We will all experience the best and worst life has to offer, based on our experience and understanding. But few understand all experiences.

Third person speech allows for one to set themselves free. So lock yourself in, by using first person opinion, as free speech.

Disappointment, is something encountered in everyday life, in all forms, yet we survive. But the fight for life, cannot conclude the same.

We all have a right to a home, so let it be each to his own. But the earth is only one, governed by the same life giving sun.

We should learn to honour those that saved our lives, not only through medicine and might. But also through art, in all its forms.

Honour should not be determined by interests, and bravery should not be governed by a criteria.

Determination can be the sole cause, for both destruction and salvation. Be wise with determination.

A journey may be taken by one. But its lessons will teach many.

Programming isn't the only form of code. One must remember how to utilise language as code. For it's always the thought that generates both.

Through folklore, we have the world of traditions today. But we must never allow for traditions, to destroy a better folklore of tomorrow.

There is no difference in benefiting many at the expense of a few, or a few at the expense of many. They are both evil, unless all benefit.

Hate was never a natural emotion within us. It's a creation, that is necessary to retaliate upon anger with revenge. Love was always natural.

It is important to know, that to believe is more vital than to know. Only through belief of a few, many today know what they know.

Knowledge can only be power, when the information is correct. Incorrect information, only causes false knowledge. One day deemed powerless.

Do not always go against what your body is telling you. But you should neither always listen. Because, only you, know your own spirit.

It is wise at times to postpone many things in life. But, it will never be wise, to postpone the fight for life.

Never celebrate too early, nor too late. For one never truly knows, how long a celebration will last, or if there will be anymore.

Destiny is not always in our hands, and sometimes we hold the destiny of another. But other times, destiny will not be understood by any.

Sometimes, it will not be understood immediately, and other times we do not approach it correctly. But, we must always pursue what is right.

Our existence within existence, baffles me. Not because I can't see the truth, but because I can't explain it through words.

Many people pray for an Angel, but few people recognise the Angels already among them. So do not always look up, sometimes look beside you.

We all live through the past. But many never really know the future, because they are always living in the present.

We usually separate from an organised body because of conservatism. Only to create our own type of conservatism.

We are all supernatural. Some listen to that which they receive more than others though, and 'few' are able to send to many consciously.

The only common belief system that has ever existed on Earth, is business. Even that though, is full of denominations.

The only time there can be true international law, is under one government.

Numbers from there, politics from there, philosophy from everywhere, beliefs from below and above. But yet, we apply it all here.

Capitalise on your own injustice and find strength in democracy. Seek peace in socialism, truth through Liberty, and you will find freedom.

Forgiveness is the most crucial factor, as to why many of us live in a civilised manner. But, don't forgive once, you see the uncivilised.

Double standards have always existed. Necessity of justice at times. But it shows, that higher standards are yet to completely exist and coexist.

Sometimes you don't have to shoot the messenger, you just have to take down the message.

They are the future, of our past. But their destiny, depends on our "present". Children.

To believe in the divine, is a freedom we are entitled to. But to know of the divine, is a moment we await.

Sometimes in order to survive another day, we must downplay the immorality of life. Other times, it seems many must become immoral to save many lives.

No spiritual journey can be easy if you've lived a materialistic life, and understanding materialism cannot be easy, if you live spiritually.

The mind is an extension of ones spirit. If you are able to remove yourself from physical corruption, you may just witness spiritual magic.

If air itself can be used as an energy source, so too, can all toxic fumes and emissions. Without removing the use of oils and gases.

There a few things in life, that can make the soul come alive, like that of a great beat, accompanied by great lyrics, in a great song.

Hundreds of millions will admire songs full of imagination. But speak of this imagination, and you will not be admired. So remember to sing.

It is wiser to place the truth in a science fiction story, for you're admired for it's creativity. Than it is to speak of it as non fiction.

Everything we have known, has been a competition. Which is a good thing, except, when that which is better, does not always prevail.

One act of courage can save the world.

A persons life cannot be compressed into a short story or a movie. For it requires selectivity, and truth is always much longer.

History is not written by the victors. But it is the writers, who pave the way for the victory.

The clouds will always form, but they will never look the same. Yet, they will always produce the same results.

A few words will be enough to start a revolution, and it will always take too many, to come to an acceptable solution.

What is good for one, can possibly hurt another.

There has never been one way of governing people, and therefore, there will always be many types of battles.

If we all believed in the creator, we would understand his decisions. But since we don't, it's hard to understand our own.

We all enter the same door into existence. But we never open the same doors through its journey. Yet the last one is again the same.

We must accept the reality, that we will never see absolute justice prevail. Not because we don't wish for it, but because it's not possible.

Striving for justice, does not always mean one is aiming for acceptance. But to only seek acceptance, one must set aside true justice.

The oppressed have always fought out of their struggles. But today, we judge oppression, by our own desires and interests, and not by truth.

There is an unspoken universal law. That which thinks freely, will be bound by no other universal law.

Not all that flies, requires wings. Not all that moves quickly, requires speed. Not all that is in motion, is moving. Use your minds.

We are generally influenced by those we see or know. But to influence, you must show others, what no one can see and what nobody knows.

Do not always fly with the wind. Because it will never tell you where it is going. But do not always go against it either. It may guide you.

We always seek a physical connection through the languages spoken in nature. Refusing to acknowledge, that the spirit always speaks louder.

For most, they must speak out to be heard. For few though, through silence, they will say much more. It is not only the ears that listen.

One who does not experience a connection with an animal will not understand its secrets. One who does not listen closely, will stay blind.

Perhaps not everyone is in tune with the reality that exists beyond our advanced world. But fine tuning this, can prove much more powerful.

Health and safety is a priority that has reshaped most of the world. But our very own unhealthy planet should be our major safety concern.

The universe is full of life and secrets. But how can we dream of exploring it, if we still haven't accepted the secrets to life on Earth.

Sometimes we must sacrifice what we thought we could never let go. But other times, we should never let go, what is too worthy of sacrifice.

We weigh ourselves by our weight. But if we were able to weigh all of our emotions throughout life, the galaxy would not be able to bear it.

It was only through imagination, that we have the world we have today. So be not scared to imagine. Just be wise, who you share it with.

Irony is a part of everyday life. We complain of water shortages, and rising seas simultaneously. Perhaps irony means change.

Sometimes we complicate language, not because we have the correct answer, but as a distraction from the answer we do not have or know.

Is a quote quotable, if the quote was quoted, when quoting a quote, was the same as other quotes. Or is the quote just making a point.

Perhaps our understanding of life depends too much on what we know and how we view ourselves. After all, the sun is alive.

It is better to be politically incorrect, and apply the right politics. Then to be politically correct, and apply the wrong politics.

It is neither a cruel world nor a cruel destiny. It is only cruel intentions, followed by cruel revenge.

It seems that we're predestined to not be allowed to think of many topics, and those who think of one, are not allowed to think differently.

The Lightning will strike downwards, but is never completely straight. Which suggests that this energy is all around us all the time.

The physical beings inhabiting the world, are an energy that does not always move straight. Therefore, direction, does not limit any energy.

The forces that we cannot see, is noticeable by too many. But there are too many, that deny our right to speak of such forces.

Real world solutions is what everyone speaks about. But we seem to deny the entirety of the real world.

If all thoughts could be transferred into words, than not all actions would take place.

Do we choose to avoid that which is not always possible to be proven, because we cannot accept that we do not know everything.

Deja vu is similar to a connection to another dimension. A world that exists, parallel to ours. Many have all experienced it, yet most deny its presence.

Many people have seen their future and many have been warned in their dreams. A dream cannot be just a dream.

A force within nature is just an energy being directed in a manner not understood. But all energy and force, can be redirected so understood

In a moment we can resolve an issue between two people. But it takes time to heal that of two or more people's.

Some things are said, that many will not feel affects them. But some things those people do, they don't realise is affecting us all.

Even though many have laid down their arms, they have not laid down their intent.

We seek justification for almost all our actions. But without justification, we also cannot act.

Sometimes when you love someone, you can say the wrong words, but feel the right things.

Without perfection and truth, life would not be. But without life, we could not seek perfection nor truth.

When man has judged you unjustly, and the other side reacts in your favour. Then you know, that mans judgment was not righteous.

Judgment day is not that which befalls us all simultaneously. But that which befalls the individual, in their place in time.

Some things are hard to explain, and others are not worth explaining.

Equality has always been the hardest fight.

We become very selective for our own ideals and perspectives. But we rarely select that which can benefit us all.

It is always the right time for the right things.

Love should never be limited. If it exists within a group, then it is powerful enough to exist anywhere.

Some things may are appear as stating the obvious, but what if the obvious is not put into practice and it is good. It must be repeated.

There can be no Husband without a Wife. No King without a Queen. No Emperor without an Empress.

Inspiration will not always be found in where you're searching. Sometimes you are just running away from where it always was. Yourself!

Some look for answers through horoscopes, maths, science, Philosophy, the creator. But some just seek food, so that their prayers will be answered.

All people have a national hero who stood up to a villain. It's ironic though, that we never portray our own villains, or another's hero.

In each, there is a David and a Goliath. We tend to not understand which one is to be utilised, and when.

Not every success story is embedded with wealth. So many, unfortunately, are of those escaping wealth. It is these stories that teach us something different.

We have come a long way forward, since slaves built the pyramids. But went way backwards, by forgetting who saved those slaves.

The greatest weapon has always been the word. It is the word. It will always be the word, and, it is we who speak the words.

The Earth is everyone's safe home. But not everyone enjoys a safe place in their home.

You cannot always succeed in having a go, but you can never fail in trying.

If we organise ourselves in a state of hierarchy on earth, as a natural state, would this same principle not apply in the universe, as we are of the universe.

It's sad, that most doctors will tell family that prayer is a final resort for saving a life. But it's power is not legally recognised.

The confusing part about spiritualism, is not that it can't be utilised, it's just that it always chooses and is bonded with the body.

We tend to attribute the obvious to coincidence. But if we all share the same air, our interconnection, was always designed to be noticeable.

To truly understand law, one must not only understand what is written, but also, what has never been spoken.

Some go through many years of schooling to earn their doctorate. Some spend all their life, so that many could become doctors.

Sometimes the voice you hear will be in distress, but it only takes moments of glory, for that voice to save all if heard correctly.

Forgiveness is a word used like no other. But its action, is rarely visible. We seem to never forget and never forgive.

Sometimes we endure injustice. But sometimes it is better to leave it where it was, because by reacting, much more injustice can occur.

We obviously need people in all sections of life. But there are those sections that need fixing, which we all rely upon.

What future do we hope to leave our children, if we become the children that took everything away from ourselves.

We have never been alone, but we have always treated our lives as if we were the only ones.

In order to save the day, we must be aware of the darkness we have placed ourselves in. For there will always be light.

If we do not begin to reverse the damage we as a collective world have caused, we will reach a point of no return. Now is time for heroes.

The Earth is like our collective heart. Always pumping life for us. But have we become its cancer and placed it on life support.

There can never be a book that will teach us everything. That is why we accompany any book, with further teachings.

In reality, we're meant to be the happiest planet in existence. Through theory though, do we all agree.

In a way we are scared to believe that there are those with supernatural abilities. Only because we are not sure of their intent.

We tend to try and make sense of facts and fiction. But sometimes fiction, offers more facts, but facts that can't be proven easily.

Synchronicity can be one of two things. That which we don't understand, or that which we do not accept.

If those who wished to control everything must still fight individuals, then they admit to fighting a power beyond their control.

I didn't create the system, or design the world. But I've accepted my place in the design of the system. But I've seen what works outside it.

If you have endured injustice all your life, and survived, further injustice only seems to become a normality. You will survive again.

Sometimes the best thing to do is not to try and prove something. But observe the consequences, as only some can understand this proof.

Heaven may not be what all believe, it may be only what some think they see, but we can't do it alone, for it is they who will set us free.

Through good and evil, injustice and righteousness, love and hate. We must all understand, we are blinded by the same fate.

There are many fighting over our following. But he who does not ask for this, is the one we must follow.

When someone proves their ability to govern a section of the world, others wish to prove that they can knock them off, at any stage they get.

A true King is not one who seeks the crown, but one who seeks to place one upon all, except himself.

We always seek justification in order to destroy something good. We wait like hyenas, for when the back is turned, to strike.

You may be the only one to teach many something that is right, but when you stop that teaching, you become the only one who is wrong.

In this world there is uncivilised torment. Then there is civilised torment. We have turned a blind eye to both.

The sun always shines, no matter what side the earth is facing it. The truth always exists, not matter how we choose to see it.

Many will attack, because they believe they have support. But when they are on the defence, you see their true face.

To be prejudice towards anything, is proof, that one lacks understanding.

What appears to be hate at times, may just be anger built up over time. So do not judge what you think you know. For you too will be judged.

We have the power to change the world. We always did. It just depends on which power we use, and what change we seek!

Science should have become the equivalent to water and air. But instead, it's like a snake, we are not sure whether it's poisonous or not.

There have already been those days that prove the creator exists. Just because we remove the proof, doesn't mean it didn't happen.

Sometimes it would be easier if we designed a social site to portray our thoughts accompanied with feelings. It would blow our minds and expand our hearts.

If we followed the life of one person, and saw the pain they endured, and watched them grow and stay strong. How do we react, or have we already reacted.

Sometimes the most important thing is to first learn about one to understand them. Not through therapy, but through truth and friendship.

Strength is not always determined by how much you can lift, or how far you can run. But strength can be, simply, how many lies one can bare.

Writing in 3rd person is the beauty in writing. Because we are able to express ourselves without revealing ourselves.

Love is blind at times because we see too much. But sometimes if we don't look, it can be us who are blind to love.

It comes to no surprise that we tend to find comfort in a book or movie. Unlike life, there always seems to be an ending worthy of our time.

We tend to waste all of our trust and belief in those undeserving of it, and forget how to trust and believe when the right ones come along.

Destiny is not always and only determined by ourselves. But it is we who have so much influence over destiny.

Most fight a war on one front, but few dare to challenge all fronts. The greatest wars have always been fought with and because of words.

Sometimes it can take for you to crumble and break apart, so that you are able to put yourself together properly.

For some, we are judged before we are born, but for all, we are judged in the end.

It is not said without reason to seek the advice of multiple opinions. After all, most also differ in values and understanding reality.

If it happens once, it's usually a coincidence or anomaly. But if it's happening everyday, it's either a conspiracy or something better.

To have a desire to accomplish the impossible, is to have will, that is not delusional.

Sadness can not always be seen on the outside, but the happiness on the inside can not be seen either.

Perhaps, if throughout history, all people had another person to lean on, we wouldn't find the need to lean towards a higher power. But life is so.

We are all so different. But it is always important to remember, that we all eat what the farmer grows.

The media is not a modern invention. It has just evolved from the days of old. Through technology, everything has just simply evolved.

The greatest resource a nation will always have is its people. For without the people, nothing is possible. People make nations great.

Is it more important for a leader of a democratic nation to be of a particular belief, or is it more important that they believe in people.

For a politician to succeed, it is not who's interests they support, but how they manage to deal with all interests, that support us.

Social values, are not determined by how you treat only your own people. But how you protect your people when being mistreated.

Every leader was chosen by the people surrounding them. But not all people, chose those who surrounded them.

Democracy may not exist as the choice of governance for all nations. But only through democratic values, can someone truly govern a nation.

What may be a mystery to many, there will always be one to whom it is a part of normal life, and it is usually they, who become the mystery.

Time spent alone, is not for all loneliness, and time spent with others, can make some feel lonely.

Sometimes a man is forced to work anything just to feed his family. But we are rarely aware of what wonders lie in such a man.

A philosopher will not duplicate his words based on another. But will portray their own, through their observation and experience.

We come across perfection through words. If we collected all the worlds perfection through words, we would have a universal masterpiece.

No atheist will ask the blood bank if the blood is from a believer, and no believer will ask if their new heart is from an atheist.

If our purpose was just to live and die. Than what allowed our thoughts to believe in the afterlife, and of things greater than us.

Why do we target those that ask questions that have never been asked, but do not provide answers to these questions.

With all the natural catastrophes caused during our life time, none has done more damage, than that caused by humanity.

There are those who save lives daily for many years. But then there are those who commit themselves for many years in order to save lives.

There has never been one person who can prove something alone. We have always required others in helping our cause. Help is essential.

Is it a waste of time, in trying to explain something to someone they don't understand, or are we wasting time if we don't just try harder.

It is the invisible force and connection between two living beings, that is sufficient proof that not all things can be proven through fact.

Behaviour viewed from the outside will not always be understood, because of what is on the inside of those who behave in such a way.

You will not always find salvation in formal education. But what you seek, can be found in a poem, song and any other piece of art.

Sometimes it is best not to respond to a fool, but then sometimes, by not responding, in the eyes of the fool, it is you who is so.

Would the appearance of the creator, stop the theory of evolution? Or would the theory "evolve"?

Schrodinger demonstrated that through science the spirit can be brought to visible life, in theory. But in reality, science unfortunately denies the spirit, or the non-physical phenomena.

A man without a soul or spirit, is a man who is restricted to understanding truth. For the soulless, anything soulful, becomes nonsense.

Sometimes to find the truth, we must read between the lines, other times, read backwards. But mostly, listen to that which does not speak.

Do we underestimate the powers of the elements, because not all of us can work with them, or we don't want those that can, to work them.

Is confusion really the same for all. Or is it a product of design for some, and a lack of understanding for the rest.

The creator is a touchy subject for everyone. Interpretation, (non)belief, law etc. But what should be more touchy, is where else can we live.

Admitting to a mistake is not the problem. The problem is that if you admit once, you are expected to admit for what is not your mistake.

Wisdom is not something that can be taught. Yet, wise traits can be learned. Wise words can be spoken, but wise action will not always follow. Making wisdom in its entirety, rare.

Is love truly understood. One will nurture and grow a vegetable with love, whilst one just loves to eat that vegetable.

Understanding, truly is the most important factor within life. Through it, one understands not only faith, but why so many are faithless.

Dramatization has become such a norm within society, that we have forgotten the necessity of reducing friction and increasing productivity.

Once upon a time, the hero carried a sword. Then it was a pen. Today it is perhaps a keyboard.

Everyone is entitled to their opinion. But we are usually faced not with 7 billion opinions, but those that are promoted most efficiently.

Are we scared to challenge that which is set before us, because we are scared to be different, or because we are scared not to be accepted.

There are many who find a fascination in an area of expertise. But there are not that many who challenge these areas of expertise.

It is not about discrediting a theory. It is about not discrediting that which created us.

As the strongest genes are suggested as being a main factor in evolution. All should have possessed the power in arms of primates.

Unfortunately we are limited to the words that we can use. Not because we don't speak the truth, but because the truth is not always accepted.

Telepathy is a word accepted in dictionaries. But it's original need to be created is neither studied nor accepted in modern times.

One who learns and reads all their life, without recognition of a certificate, can teach as much as one who gains a certificate on one topic.

We tend to pay close attention only to those with a recognised paper. Without recognising that our knowledge, originally comes from those without paper.

A long explanation can sometimes bring forth too many questions, but a short explanation, can redefine many answers.

There are many examples in nature that demonstrate a non physical connection between life forms.

On the outside we all look the same. On the inside we all share the same properties. But deep within, only few understand our connection.

Faith through the understanding of religion has always caused immeasurable damage, not of its own fault. But faith itself, can create immeasurable understanding.

There have been many people that have changed our world. But there have been many more people who have made these changes happen!

Technology will not be the cause if we were to stop using our minds. But the lack of progress within technology.

Sometimes we must speak in code, not because we are hiding, but because the same thought without code, can lead to the wrong conclusions.

We can never be accepted or loved by all. Usually, because we are not understood. But if one learns to not hate, then we can understand them.

A positive moment can arouse the most pleasant of thoughts, but a negative one can bring forth the most positive of moments.

We can not always expect acknowledgment for our success by others, but if you have helped others in succeeding, then acknowledge yourself.

The sun shines even when it is dark.

The wise will know when to speak and when not to. But the brave will speak the truth even when it is not wise. Making truth, the wisest at times.

We tend to dwell on what we determine to be reality. Forgetting that we are all descendants of those that once only had a stick for a tool.

When one has overcome the pressures of life, through understanding the reality they have been placed in, the realities others see, change.

Happiness is sometimes found in writing. Not because one can play with words, but because ones truest feelings are never a game.

The greatest of men can speak the wisest words, but those not considered as great, can demonstrate the greatest wisdom.

Each person has played their role in this world, some bringing forth negativity, others positivity. But inside, we all seek acceptance.

Some people specialise in one field, and some are awoken by many. But few understand the power of love, and the many doors it can open.

Words can at times be too much, and other times they are not enough. But the right words, at the right time, will always be sufficient.

Sometimes we don't have to prove what not all can see. Sometimes we just have to feel it, to understand what another has seen.

The feelings and emotions one feels, is something that is beyond the physical self. One can not measure the pain or love through the body.

Without powerful science, productive study in biology and chemistry, we will never be able to understand our full potential, or our meaning.

With the millions of stories over thousands of years of people witnessing spirits, does one attribute this to evolution, or something more?

Truth has been spread through religion, science, philosophy. Never allowing for its unification. Causing division and confusion among us.

There has always been intellectual evolving. But isn't it interesting that we have yet to manage to spark this evolution in modern apes!

There is a universal law that governs creation of all life.

Some of the lightest things in the universe, are the hardest burdens to carry.

Harvest the light, that was bright. Harvest the night, that was might. Harvest the truth, that was proof. But the numbers 123, that was free.

To know the truth of something or many things, is to be part of something or someone. Yet, to be accepted as someone, is not always easy.

What is an idea, but a thought. What is a thought, but energy. What is energy, everything.

The entrance of any library, should have written, "Can you see what I see". If not to be added, then to be taught upon entry.

It is not only the words used that matter, it is the words not used, that also matter.

Alpha Bee, to much honey, glide it through the wind, without hurry.

Claws grabbed tight, voice went silent, thoughts rush like lightning, but he raises the light, and the dark wolf goes away.

Sometimes it's hard not to say something, and other times it's hard to say. So, one must either finish what they are saying, or not start at all.

It's those who have made unintentional mistakes that try to fix them, and not those that make intentional mistakes. All is set when all is angled.

It is possible to keep all in the angles, by keeping all bodies away. For it's the presence of the body, that will remove itself from the angles.

Anyone knows how hard it is for an individual to maintain a belief all life long, without alterations. Imagine centuries, and many people.

As science is a language, already set in existence, which people are still yet 2 truly understand. It is possible to preach through science.

Who understands, will get it. "One can be made to do what others do, sometimes. But can others do, what that one can do, any other time".

A promise yes, a deal no, so what's the deal, to say a promise. A promise will last forever, a deal must always reach an end.

Anyone in this world describing themselves through one word, has either not woken up, or does not understand that this world offers much more.

It is better to work with a gift, than to work the gift. A gift can only be unwrapped once, and worked too hard, wrapped up once.

Existence is One. Therefore, all is one ultimately. What hurts one, will hurt all. But few have seen this uniquely over time, allowing progress for all.

Without existence, no comments would exist. Seems all should be grateful. Philosophy is not for all, because in philosophy, one must use thought.

In the end, one can't expect everyone to respect or like another. But if what they say, see, show, is what you dream of. What is more important.

To be for something, does not mean to be against anything else.

Through time, all have been enemies and all have been friends. The enemy of the enemy, and the friend of the friend, have been shared by all.

There was one who took his time. Read all that he could. It was a lot in comparison to others. One day he understood them, they never could him.

When one insists their mind on saying something, they can't hear what is said back. Because they don't listen, they will never see.

It is better to cry, than through anger to cause damage. It is better to rain, than for the storm to take it all away.

Both a wise, and not so wise person will remain quiet, appearing the same. But once they start to speak, anyone can tell wisdom from what is not.

When love is stronger than hurt or pain or anger, moving forward, is easy. When understanding joins love, it's a walk in the park.

Back and forth, it set itself free. Yet freedom it was not, the noise was a lot. Teachings and signs plenty, easy, but peace was no where.

How are there people out there, that find it easier to cry for others, than to see others cry in front of them.

Ironically it's the earth that looks at the universe as lifeless. But imagine it was looking back at a living planet killing life.

Good people carry the weight of those who can't. A mother for a child. A father for a child. Siblings for siblings, a being for a being, and around again.

Most things are harder to do, than to say. But sometimes it's the hardest to say, because it's been said the first time.

Search for the good in the bad, so the bad knows of it, and search for the bad in the good, so the good knows of it. This way, goodness maintains its rotation.

Only through understanding can one love. Emphasis is on the understanding, and not how much is understood. Each finds it on their own, so too love.

That which seeks destruction for another, has in such a way, began the process of self destruction. The opposite is also true.

If one finds a correct answer after a mistake, than the mistake served only as progression. But it is different, if the mistake is the last answer.

One will always be able to survive on only bread crumbs, no matter how much wheat there is. No one should ever throw away their bread crumbs.

We live in an existence, in which understanding of the word infinity, is ever present, beyond all we see. Infinity, maintains hope eternally.

If hope is not in all, and hope is not for all, than the hope is not at all.

If the body had no mind, but was mechanical, a moment, would only be that moment. But because of the mind, that body and moment have no time in space.

People have fought and died for their companions. Most other people will wonder once through life, why. But in a world of man, only that friend can.

It's the capability of thought, which makes people learn. It's not reading that solely teaches one. There's plenty that all read, yet few understand.

Whether it's good or evil, it requires people.

If one does not feel all feelings, how could one understand life. On a daily basis, occupations bring about all things. Yet no one is defined by it, or rather, should not be.

No great person came to be instantly, without time and investment, from many during growth. All progress inevitably quickens, but once grew slowly.

To see it, for how it really is, & not the opposite, is rare these days. It always will be, "1 small step for mankind, & 1 giant leap for man".

They that do not know, read. They that know, write. But one who always reads and writes, will always keep knowing.

What further proof must be needed throughout time, than that of how far we have progressed, to realise, limits have been our own doings.

To know something, it must not be thought, to again be considered. But to think about something, it is then, not yet completely known.

Not a thing that can't be summarised, however complicated. Problem lies in explanations, which no longer make it summarised, but complicated.

One must keep in mind, almost entirely, everyone alive, lives a life they didn't choose. This creates illusions of alter ego's. But it's survival.

For every life choice, hobby, occupation, destination, family, pets etc, there is someone, for whom it is a waste of time and life without purpose. But that should not take your meaning away.

Everything that exists wants to be explained. But not everything in existence, wants everything else to be explained. Wise explanation, is increased power.

Not a thing in existence, that can't be explained. A thought, a vision, sight, sound, smell, touch and ability for total awareness, makes us at the forefront of life.

The problem is not deep thought, or overthinking. Only such a way, has anything positive even been propelled from the thought, to the ground. The problem lies in, not stepping back every so often.

It is better to remain a friend with someone long distance, and a helping hand at all times, than to spend too much time together, and become enemies.

Years of life combined, each segment from one another would divide, making all the information multiplied, and the unknown becomes sciences, applied.

Nothing is ever just for one person, nor does one do something, just for themselves. Ultimately all for one, is for all, and one for all, is ultimately also for all.

The more pressure, prejudice, focus and obstacles one encounters in life just for survival, could never serve as a negative aspect for the revival.

Being different, doesn't mean not being normal. What is not normal, becomes fashion, style, culture. To be the same and normal, is what will make you feel different.

No progress began in a comfort zone. Yet, a comfort zone may be offered to complete the progress.

It's possible to be rude, yet still be polite. But it seems to be, that politeness, is the rudeness, and rudeness is politeness at times.

For some things, only few have raw experience. Only few, than really know such experience. Yet, even fewer, will also have open minds, for the latter.

Something that cannot be done fast, must be done slowly. But not all things.

Music can temporarily lose someone, through enjoyment. Yet, without music, all could be lost.

The feedback, just another one. Still paying, when it's done. Feedback, like second to none, and even feeding it back, appearing a lot of fun.

I think, for any good person to have lived a life, one must have called a family member a friend, and a friend, a family member.

There is nothing that can define me, but it is I that defines all things surrounding me. With the exception, that as I, people are not things.

For all things, only precise reasoning, can become proof, where all other proof, is lacking. Yet, ironically, few understand what reasoning is.

There is no complete task, if all attaching information was not considered.

Interesting to think, that for most people, animals are less 'evolved, yet their abilities and senses, is what we'd find only in science fiction production.

There have been created, by people, many stereotypes about our own world, that what isn't second nature, seems to have devolved into many more.

It seems to be rare and forbidden, or rare, because it's forbidden, or seems forbidden, because it's rare, to have all that one needs, but what one needs, is not much at all.

An updated version, always brings forth results much faster than an outdated version. The same is true for the information, stored in our books.

Thoughts, dreams, and desires, would never have the same beauty, if it were not for description through language, and languages are plentiful.

The truth never has to be proven, it just has to be clarified.

He carries the radio, spreads out its hands, picking up the signals, switching between bands, noting the truths, and how all actually stands.

Search far and wide, all that's inside, put nothing aside, information travels through a tide, truth when lied, no way to hide, quantum must be tried.

If the universe and existence were not awake, we would not even be alive.

Share your thoughts, with all you see, but many are confused, by a mind that's free, so be wise and yet open, use words to calm but do not plea.

The mountain drools, collects along the way, the air unites it, clouds have their say, earth is calm, it doesn't play, existence awakes, playing with clay.

A circle drawn, with space around, stretched far and wide, yet staying close and sound, through complete simplicity, nothing that can't be found.

The same thing can be both overrated and underrated. It just depends, what position you observe it from, and what situation you observe it in.

A person is only as open, alive, present, as what they learn through life. The moral is to never stop learning.

Hate is the greatest setback, in one truly expanding their own mind, and finding out their own limits.

Someone who does not see infinite and believes not in the impossible, will never be able to discover, see and contemplate existence, the same way those that do.

One doesn't always have to know how to explain something to know that they know it. But there are too many explaining, what they don't really know.

I know everything that I know. I can learn everything that I need to know.

Everything in the world has always been perfect, except for people.

The depth great philosophers go into, is one hallmark, that the entire universe would be proud of, as it ventures into what few know.

What is proof, and who decides, what is truth, when taking sides, decisions made, upon who presides, perception lies, from all them prides.

The truth is. Many can be given large swathes of money, and basic progress is made. Yet, few can be given, very little, and all the possible progress is made.

Nature has never brought forward anything by accident. People have never placed anything without intention. Still, no one can play the creator.

Once something enters existence, it has existed, therefore, it was, is and always will be. Humanity, only due to choices, lives down the order.

Even a burned form of energy turned into smoke, is still forever energy. Examples are plentiful. Air being the best. One must understand, that invisibility, does not mean obsolete.

There are few people, who understand consequences for all, and therefore refrain from actions, many others would consider irrelevant. But many others understand.

A meaning deeper than the words actually stated. If one does not leave what is trying to pull them down, than they will never rise.

Those who have reached the furthest intellectual places throughout history, did so, with their own understanding, abilities and mind.

There is a simple formula to trust. It goes with help. By allowing one freedom, to demonstrate how they help, one will know whether to trust or not.

Humanity has too many times drifted towards what appears to be most enticing for the eyes. Forming what most think, humans should be now. But our nature, was to nurture nature.

Anything that exists, spiritual or not, must always have a physical presence within existence, as it exists. As such, with our physical presence, a dream is then physical also.

Do not be fooled by the stereotypes that have been made the norm. A vegetable feeds the largest land mammal, but also grows extremely quick.

We are part of and from nature'. Ironically, it's always those few that are known for their connection with nature, and not those for their disconnection.

A reaction by those without the tools or knowledge towards something particular, that hasn't been brought to a conclusion, always backfires.

Sometimes one must appear to have a cold heart towards one human being, to be able to help all humanity. For everything, there is a sacrifice that must be made.

There are many questions, not asked, because most aren't aware they even exist. The answers, therefore, can only be answered by a few.

One does not have to fight hard to read, for it requires only minimal effort. But to think and to write, sometimes one must fight an inner battle.

There simply isn't any progress if everyone and everything is the same. Yet, those that are different, making difference, are ridiculed mostly.

Can you remember, what you thought, when you said, what another brought, are you connected, with yourself, or are you chosen, off the shelf.

Humanity is leading on one of two paths. Near mastering technology and removing nature, which turns its back. Or, respecting nature through technology.

When one truly unravels in a single moment truths within existence to themselves. Then they realise that all good life is to be celebrated and no tears of sadness flow.

Why is it, that it seems to be normal, that it is a greater evil to be angered by evil committed by another, than the actual evil, committed by the other.

There is no such thing as 50% faith or even 99%. It is 100% or it means nothing.

When a prejudice is put into place, and truth buried deep, than it's only natural, that through process, that prejudice appears here and there.

It wasn't the world which enabled the creativity and truth to come alive, from the injustice, theft and hardship. It was the individual themselves always.

There's no need to push someone away that chooses to go. But, the fool is he who thinks, they can reverse a situation, to claim righteousness.

Too many opinions, are the cause of so much lost truth and so many false stories. That is why, any serious group, leaves it to a few for each case.

Most important lesson never acknowledged by the majority of humanity. Is that the children have been teaching the parents all their lives.

Individuals turned into religion, and signs as holy possessions. Meant to represent true love, respect and honour, yet many who wear them, contradict them.

Of all words, success is one that has no correct definition. But to succeed through self concentration in reaching the unimaginable, is cool.

Perhaps the truly single hardest thing in life, is to have seen perfection, but to live in an imperfect world.

Zoning in. But never changing. Learning more. Information rearranging. People less confused. Life is not for staging. Then we see. The existence I'm paging.

They never asked for anything in return, yet their understanding and help was beyond belief. The close played the good, but the far, help shine the light.

He who does and thinks evil, sees the entire world as evil, and then, teaches the young the evil ways. The same is true for the good, but for some reason show too much vigilance.

It must be. Not because it had to be. But choices of others forced it to be. Not all must be. But like a democratic election. People choose it.

It's been said, too many times, truth scrambled, through many rhymes. Stories told, beliefs rise, could never handle, the honest surprise.

Truth is, man couldn't handle the presence of what it sustains only through statues. But requires the power of that name, to build institutions.

It couldn't be done, not by one, not by two, or a few, it's been tried, many times, every turn, treated as crimes, but just to try, that one will forever fly.

When the Kingdom of life senses a good soul, it helps, befriends, and stands for. When the kingdom of man senses. One never knows what to expect.

The tricks of the trade, by man they're made, but the universe stayed, for those that prayed, game never played, from goodness never swayed.

Only man steps out of order among nature. Only man goes against the very nature it belongs to. Only man hasn't learned it's own given teachings.

What's the test, and who's it for, when mistakes are made, to even a score. When it should be, equal for all, the choices made, should not make things stall.

I lived, I did live, I'm alive.

We see much beauty, judged by the individual. But music, is a beauty we see with a sense we can't describe, yet, we think we only hear it.

The blueprints are there, for all that is necessary to bring forth great changes.

Reversing the truth, and arguments, will bring forth large consequences. The small minded, who see not the big picture, should first learn.

Words need to be created to describe something. But how can definitions be put together by those who haven't experienced what only few have.

One must grasp the difficulty others face in this life to understand them. Certain individuals, have always had the ability to balance what others cannot. This balance, has and always will be fought within the individual themselves, and others will never understand.

One with a gift, has no sides. But the gifted, is always pulled to all sides.

One who shows no forgiveness, is hard to be approached. One who does, in the eyes of others, has given a premature green light, to always be attacked. Which one must change.

All forces and powers strive to learn as much as possible, believing that through collection of knowledge they know all. Until proven wrong.

There is one truth never to be taught, but psychologically, those with a deep understanding of this subject know. The truth is hard to grasp.

To conspire and set up an unnatural situation to draw attention to a wider audience, only shows the personality and character of those who conspire.

A soul/consciousness spread through existence. Separated from itself, only to grow, and learn, and eventually coming together, as large as life.

The only mysteries that exist, are the ones we are not willing to learn about. The ones who are willing to learn everything, know only reality.

Some people were born great in their own rights. If you add, or pick too much at that person. You may never receive everything on offer.

Sometimes few are given things no one else has. Money, is a form of trade, meant to bring civility to the worlds population. But many realise in life, not everything can be purchased.

False remark, bounces back, false intention, allows for others to track, a hard truth is better to back, than continue falsely, where all will slack.

Things can be done easily. Avoiding it all, appears intelligent. Denying truth, appears wise. But being accepted, is only for the brave.

Just because someone cannot or does not admit to something, however small or grandiose, it doesn't mean that it's not true and that it did not happen.

A mind at ease, keeps the body still, and a mind not, never looks real, not all think, but all can feel, few move all, and all know it's real.

A mind, is not able to concentrate at such a high level, if it has done wrong. Such a mind fights only because it has been wronged.

Energy is simply part of creation as we ourselves are. Without us, energy could not be understood, and without energy, nothing would be the same.

Are the words unspoken, louder than the voice, is each word spoken, completely of our choice, is it help or confusion, in which all rejoice.

An individual, that is good in heart, will be good for, and through any religion, because the individual is good. All good individuals know this, and for this reason are at peace.

What isn't wild, can't be tamed. What was naturally always meant to be wild(free), should not be tamed. Freedom was a birthright.

All great ideas that were yet to be understood, were always deemed grandiose for the vast majority, except for the one, who's idea it was.

There is no true understanding of energy without having faith, and there is no true ability in expressing faith, without understanding energy.

Being angry at the evil deeds and intentions of others continuously isn't evil. One should always remember, the anger is because of the evil.

One can be a target for doing good, or becoming a target for wishing no good. If a target must be placed, make sure it is for the right reason.

A different time, different place, different group, different case, different laws, different space, different game, different face.

Some peoples most intelligent moments, are intelligent peoples most stupid.

To send away, is not to stay, you've gone beyond, your lovely stay, words aren't needed, but yes you may, reversing truth, is not wise play.

A man will show the depth of his understanding through every small deed. Through every response. Through every action. Which shows the heart.

To achieve what is not achievable, in the right settings, is a great thing. To do the same, without any right setting, is not conceivable for most.

First one must learn to practice, minimum effort, for maximum results. Followed by, one maximum effort, for eternal results.

Hard to believe, and hard to accept, on this earth, some still respect. State of confusion, lack of knowledge, prejudice is blind to good, so evil they forage.

Anything invented, designed, created, and works, was always meant to be and could be. Once these were impossible, but impossible is what can't be.

All were born to plan, design, invent, engineer, speak, think, to feel, to question. But few, were designed for all this, and to create.

From self awareness, the thoughts flowed freely, fearless of the unknown, became simple really, and more it worked, more it saw clearly.

It vibrates, through invisible codes, overriding, all technological modes, inaccessible, through binary codes, out of scope, unique modes.

It's a brake one cannot apply or change, a force out of range, a denial you must rearrange, through information it's very strange, but a frequency within range.

Few accept it all, for a greater cause, never giving up, but sometimes must pause, forgetting about themselves, so that information reaches all shores.

It was always so, growing within, smile through pain, for every clue a pin, leaving a trail, so good will win, destiny maybe, but not every sin.

Energy would flow, gliding past and through everything, interferences everywhere, the truth to bring, fighting a battle, accepting each sting.

In everything is a message. In everything is good and bad. You see what your soul desires to see. But the good, is always the true message.

When people react in spite, it's anger built up through falseness, and released at the wrong people. What's sad, is that anger taught in the young.

When one desires for you to rely upon them, but isn't there, when you need them most, but you are there for them, it's time to learn to rely upon yourself.

Some people don't choose to live the hardest life by choice. What they chose, is to make the lives of others easier, and hardship followed.

People can lie. Numbers can lie. Energy, never lies.

Perhaps perfection is not possible in everyone's eyes. But it's only aiming at perfecting everything, that we can expect the best possible results in all we do.

You may receive signals, that are artificial in nature. You choose, to believe if they're right or wrong, or to follow. Divine guidance is always true.

One of the worst things parents can do to their children, is through them, be what they couldn't and do what they didn't. All have their own dreams.

Too many times people confuse anger and evil. Anger will come out of mistakes, misunderstandings, confusion, but can be forgiven. Evil cannot.

If you are willing to be defined by any name, other than by a person, you have already lost free will, freedom, free choice and a free future.

A child is free when small, but also vulnerable. It's this vulnerability that allows a child's subconscious to be absorbed and lose free will when old. But a child's will endures.

There is no puzzle that can be completed without all the pieces.

When something has to be caged. It's not the caged one who fears, but those that are caging. If the caged was peaceful outside the cage, then those who have caged, have done wrong.

As we are equal in so many ways, we are all so different. Some people dream, but some people can fulfil their dreams. Some people imagine, others have great visions.

There're many different type of people. All enjoy different degrees of extreme experiences. These memories, no one can touch, and everyone should be able to and can enjoy.

Animals(beings) have been used to save people, for many years. Many do, without asking them. People owe them, to do the same.

If the radio was not online and up and running, society and civilisation would be delayed, and progress would not be possible.

If one committed evil acts, they respond with threats, due to fear. If one committed no evil, they only respond with warnings, due to fearlessness.

There may be no such thing as an inventor. It is not because it was not invented, but rather discovered by such people. For one, cannot invent what cannot be.

There is one fundamental flaw in interpretation of life, that confuses far too many. There is only one existence.

If one was not meant to see, all that they see, then they would not see it. If one, knows what they know, they were meant to know it. Accept it or not.

It's become a weird world, in the sense that, it's not known if the intelligent one is the one that builds the tracks and train, or the one who simply jumps aboard.

The future seen, a reaction occurs, the silent wind, its power spurs, a reenergising passage, the face of hers, will of mine, the sun, moon and earth it stirs.

The physically sedentary man is not always the lazy one. It was the most sedentary who are looked upon by all cultures. Because, they found a way and peace.

Do not fry your brain young, do not let the song of pain be sung, through nature your healing will be rung, allowing to pass what has stung.

People always find it easier to believe ridiculous excuses, rather than obvious truths. Then hide from the truth, with a ridiculous excuse.

If one pays attention to those causing hurt and pain to many, and observe those saving and helping others, Perhaps they would see the difference between the good and not so good.

It was intervention, power by extension, future seen through observation, energy with contemplation, understand the motivation, and the destination.

Can you hear, or do you fear, it's not multitasking, it's simple and clear, weird becomes normal, and normal weird, just matters, the direction steered.

Similarities occurring in ancient times by cultures unaware of another, is no coincidence. No book had been all true. But many reference points are.

Formal education will seek to narrow the most relevant subjects required for a specific field of interest. Self education will expand on all.

The lime lights bright, hard to stay right, keeping sane day and night, is one tough fight, reaching a light, always in flight, test of might.

What can one do, that one can't too, slipped the clue, or sent it through, for me or you, won lost or drew, knowing who, is knowing what's true.

Coincidence here, coincidence there, coincidence everywhere, somehow there's no reason where ever you stare, but coincidentally, it's all a pair.

It's when one realises that the surface hasn't even been scratched, and yet so much is clear, that you can't even imagine, what the future beholds.

We observe the animal kingdom, and even so different, we view them as one. Yet we observe humanity, with minor differences, as aliens.

We can never all be the same on earth, it was never meant to happen. But we were meant to build a world, so all are treated equal. Can we make it.

It is never the whole world, that can change one individual. But it has always been, that one individual, can change the world.

One of the fundamental concepts that need to be grasped by every generation. In each generation, certain individuals were viewed as delusional, before being heard.

Dramatic changes are like a see saw. One will climb, the other fall, applied positively, to gradually crawl, allows sustainability, which is good for all.

To be wrong, and say it loud, is to know right, yet staying proud, not to be bothered, pleasing the crowd, knowing the bread, follows once it's plowed.

Thank you to those, who tried their way, the angels as doctors, who disregard pay, teachers of nature, their part to play, I remember, for you I pray.

You're never too young, never too small, if your dreams are real, then stand tall, if your plans are right, then you won't be allowed to fall.

A bird it is even with clipped wings. A scorpion when no longer stings. A singer when no longer sings. An angel if it continuously brings.

If by one a position is abused, then by them the position should not be used, but helping others should not be confused, if evil is being defused.

The year it was, the date differs, the scene the same, memory never withers, the rules unchanged, the source remembers, most are unaware, of all the measures.

Energy was always present, but many minds were blind, connections avoided, it was hard to find, with modernisation, we'll connect every kind.

Names applied, attention is not, teaching a lesson, the truth forgot, surrounding all, but unaware, staying deaf and blind, honesty will scare.

You cannot be part of a game, if you don't play. But you cannot avoid being part of existence, if you exist.

When one continuously keeps forgiving anyone or everyone for repetitive actions, there are only two facts. That individual has always been good, and those who must be forgiven, are not. But the positive is, such examples offer hope for all.

You cannot clean the hands, once you've caused hurt, cannot seek another to blame, once you cause the hurt, energy forgets not, no matter the shirt.

Don't apply the blame, once the act is done, being young or old, immorality causes no fun, the reactions brought forward, is because of what others have done.

Watching it all, receiving the information, hearing the mockery, but light will still glow, attached by air, all of life, we choose, eternity or strife.

Peace found inside, appears as weak, truth be told, others are bleak, not for the self, but for all others, control must be, to save sisters and brothers.

It is the law, it is the natural, a super version, always was actual, defying logic, but always real, a given opportunity, no one can steal.

In life, it's worth forgiving what is unforgivable by human standards. It's the hardest thing to do, but only the strongest can do it.

With the mind, control is true, through the mind, all comes through, natural order, my mind is blue, mind over matter, what an obvious clue.

It's always those, who seek to make the lives of others safe, that find themselves in the most unsafe situations. Rarely understood or known.

The darkness can never out power the light. For when the light is angered, the darkness disappears in a flash.

The more one knows, the more one is. The less one knows, the less one becomes. But most importantly, is the difference in how one chooses to use all of this.

Radio cannot pickup a signal, without the source sending the messages. Radios are tuned differently. Some open to am, some open to fm. But there must be at least one, open to all.

Defy the law, by bending air, or a new law, something better to bare, or old but lost, why would it scare, when universe is speaking, for what is fair.

Quick to act, when the event takes place, quick to give reason, after enduring what some face, but never wise enough, for the cause of said case.

Life is great, for many to date, not much on the plate, own world within their crate, but shouldn't create, an outside state, of a larger fate.

When there's a price, all seems nice, no rolling a dice, or thinking twice, easily bought with a slice, needing no advice, but priceless will suffice.

Perpetual motion, isn't a state that has yet to be found, for it is existence. But what continues, does not always produce the same results.

There's a difference when one ventures out, to put a puzzle together, by way of detective work. But, another thing, when the pieces are brought forward alone.

No one to sympathise, yet seeing truth so clear, but don't react, afraid by the fear, run from truth, through rum and beer, now don't facts, influence the peer.

A hero not, to turn a blind eye, a hero never, to hear an innocent child cry, a hero can't be, if one doesn't try, must a hero die, if always questions why.

Natures best, stands alone, solving problems, there is no clone, purest intentions, unbreakable stone, curable will, for flesh and bone.

Who determines the definition of the word success. Is the one who created an environment for millions to succeed, less successful than they are.

10 commandments. 1. Be good. 2 Wish good. 3. See good. 4. Search good. 5. Find good. 6. Do good. 7. Think good. 8. Love good. 9. Live good. 10. Dream good.

All things evolve as they learn more, using the mind, as has law, as has art, as has tech, as should all. But so too, should conservatism.

The limelight is bright, hard to stay right, keeping sane day and night, is one tough fight, reaching a light, always in flight, is a test of might.

In everybody's sight, controlling wind and kite, would you be alright, or endure a plight, stricken by fright, no easy bite, but we are tight.

Secrets, and knowledge, or tricks, and porridge, confused, by information, or silent, by confirmation, separate, and controlling, or is one, rolling.

You can be what you like, and freedom promoted, words left behind, meanings became bloated, so which is applied, when truth seems coated.

Everyone decides fate collectively.

There is a reverse psychological factor applied. That due to lack of knowledge, ancient beliefs were inferior. But for the natural, the opposite may be true.

There is not one place on earth, or one group of people, who haven't been taught through belief, of an after life, without knowledge by others.

Mercy is not something that is given by another. Mercy is something that is earned by the individual. It's philosophical, but energy does not lie.

The stars have always been taking care of earth through life. But no longer must anyone wait for the night, for at least one star was left for the day.

Coincidence here, coincidence there, coincidence everywhere, yet somehow there's no reason where ever you stare, yet coincidentally, all has it's pair.

It's when one understands not, a language, and does not allow for advice, claiming to know all, and leaving discretion in such hands, that can cause all else to fail.

Desire to know, ability to grow, avoiding the show, anywhere to go, appearing to think slow, making others glow, never inflicting a blow, to end the show.

There's a problem in life, if one has to try to be good. Being good, is simply to be good. Goodness has no secret definition. No excuse is valid for the opposite.

Speed life up, and little is seen, slow it down, remember where you've been, energy appeared wasted, with all in between, but direct energy, is there to learn if one is keen.

Choice it was, choice it stays, the mind alone, is a learning phase, tried it all, middle of life, and expanded more, even through strife.

The race among humanity, rarely spoken of, but feared by all. Integrated within all groups. Going by different names. They are, the Ancient good.

One should remember, that gravity is a major force within existence. But, if one jumps, they realise, that by will, even gravity can be defied.

The greatest teachers, only became great, when accompanied by the greatest of students. Only a great student, can ask great questions.

Connections are felt, both low and high, seen by us all, even energies through wi-fi. Not a spot, that one can hide, both nature and tech, appear on the one side.

1000 slices of cake. 1000 people each have a slice. 1000 different opinions. That is the definition of opinion. Such opinions are not collective facts.

Civil society should not be based on 'Agreeing to disagree', but, 'Agreeing to agree and disagree'. No united front ever agreed on all things, yet progress was possible.

Coincidence. Is it mere coincidence that everything is perfect for us to exist, and that a form of intelligence surrounds us on all sides. Or as science says, there is a reason for it all.

Another dimension, lurks around, presence of life, but rarely found, laws applied, so all is sound, not all reincarnate, if here they're bound.

A nick name, is not to blame, for the fame, or lack of the same. A given reign, abilities not plain, named by the rain, is never so bane.

There have been times, when what was told to the people, was against their interest, became the very thing, that the people fought for, as their important interest.
It is better to know more things, than more words. It's always easy to find a word for the things you need, than things for the word you need.

One great person, doesn't make a great people. One people, can't define one person. One earth, housed all people. People, only have one earth.

Symbolism, in the right direction, serves, for ones protection. Theories, apply objection, reality, offers its rejection. Many projections.

Stupidstitions perhaps, no accident, no mishaps. Cultures, survived, meanings, revived. Understanding, by few, connections, not new.

What's it like, many wondered, through songs and tales, many pondered. In glory and pain, all dreamed, in private thought, the mind beamed.

Aspire, to be everything, knowing, you'll be one thing, thing, that you'll be, determines, all you can see. Seen, what's unique, future, isn't bleak.

What's a number, but just a word, looks different, like every bird. It's simplified, to help us out, and organises, to learn about.

What is desire, what is a heart, what are emotions, that keep us apart. Connections made, none can deny, why stop truth, when all could fly.

Banjo had spoke, felt the snow, wrote through poems, understanding flow, messages encrypted, truth clear as day, he saw light, his own way.

Names change, meaning applied, future helps, decoding supplied. What's right, what's wrong, can be heard, in every song.

If all the wise people throughout history, were alive today in their respective lands, from who much understanding is owed to, they'd be known as wise guys.

The black sheep, helped the white sheep find a nice patch of grass. The white sheep then pushed the black sheep out, and said, you've stained us.

How can any ancient book be discredited, from its time, when the world was yet to unite, by uniting the information. But the laws are brought over into the present, without much objections.

We all learn, At different rates, of different things. But, sometimes, it's important to not only learn, but to remember and try to teach, what one has learned.

A test is studied for, and in many ways, so is life. One will not find all the answers by reading. But, life, offers so many signs and wonders, that it is within this, that all else can be learned.

Light is law, energy is dark. Invisible force, igniting the spark. Surpassing matter, defying laws. Proves its power, demonstrating flaws.

The metaphor, is for all, listen close, rich and poor. Words are weird, and choice is yours, by opening up, truth can enter all the pores.

Turned my back, kept on running, she kept chasing, and she was stunning. I was scared, to believe it's you, now I'm chasing, knowing it's true.

Concentration, eyes for rays, concentrated, energy stays. Concentrate, direct its ways, concentrate without delays. Concentrate, the concentration.

Roadblocks all along, obstacles make their say. Potholes make you stop, others show the way. Will can break a wrong plan, and energy helps if you pray.

May be bold, you may not be sold, but you are not told, all that's on hold, some don't fold, during the cold, what is rolled, holds what is untold.

Many things are identical with opposites. But to say, "it is never too late to do something cruel", is nothing like saying, "never too late to do good".

Days surpassed, against wrongful eyes, one had heard, the honest cries, no one foresaw, who lives or dies, cruelty had lost, through many tries.

Perhaps, the simple most greatest philosophical sign. Explained so simply. Described so simply. Drawn so simply. Yet the meaning is so large and great. Yin and yang.

Answers are simple, some are just not accepted. Few know the truth, by the credible may be rejected. Removing all prejudice, some can be respected.

From a distance, some will show hate, but from up close, the air shows fate. Not to be evil, or to abuse, but to teach all, how to calm ones fuse.

Teach ourselves, to connect to the conscious, ridding ourselves, of all nonsense, understanding, our own subconscious, letting in, all the sense.

Be straightforward, line by line, creativity is freedom, there'll be no fine. Who can read, the msgs sent, from delusions, they're absent.

To live free, dream out loud, opened minds, must be proud, share words wisely, to touch the crowd, spread the thoughts, through each sound, that way more, will be found.

A real judge, is one who has proven their ability to seek true justice. Not one fighting to be appointed, or placed to play a role. For true justice, is having true understanding to ones surroundings.

Life isn't a movie. Trust isn't so easy. But like a movie, as much as is being done behind the scenes to hurt people, there is always much done to help.

Even though humanity is not perfect. Within the vastness and entirety of existence, and its perfection, to function and hold life, all must remember, that humanity is part of that perfection.

Bird whispers, no sound is heard. Cloud rushes by, followed by the bird. Branches sway, air seems still. All are amazed, knowing it's real.

If one needs to create reasons to hate another, there was never a true reason. If one needs to create situations to anger another, there was never anger.

It will be encouraged to be the best and strongest you can be. But in this world, there are too many who fear this. So rise slowly, and do it right.

Balancing is hard. Plenty wish freedom for all. Plenty use law. Plenty use politics. Many use it all. But it truly takes time for all, to be accepted.

Diversification is the solution, so that both big and small are placed in a position to move forward and not cause a domino effect.

Water is precious, calm and clean, when isolated from the rest.

Humanity set off on all its explorations, using the power of wind, by understanding it. But then suddenly stopped.

Anyone can tell you what the weather may be like, just before it arrives, by simply glancing upwards. But no one, will tell you, how the sudden changes in wind occur.

Ideas and plans are plentiful. But too many times, humanity ends up relying on the plans of a few, so that all other plans are only acceptable, if they can be incorporated. But great plans, should never be placed aside for too long.

Laws of old, cannot always be applied in times of new. But sometimes we need ways of old, to not destroy the new times.

There is always a solution that does not destroy the pyramid structure. Some ideas, just strengthen its foundation.

Sometimes overloading data can be the cause of the problem. So it is important to use the right data, in order to find the solution.

It is not politics that was ever the problem. It is the type of politics that causes problems.

It is of irreplaceable value that we have experts in all fields, but it is more important at times, to have such individuals understand the importance of knowing the boundaries.

Sometimes we require financial backing to have our ideas heard, but sometimes, these stolen ideas, allow for them to be heard freely. Yet, the source never changes.

Constructive thought is hard to be understood by all, and philosophical thinking is the reason it becomes hard to understand.

Anyone can claim that something has been designed or written before them, but they can never claim to understand it as well.

Words can at times be too much, and other times they are not enough. But the right words, at the right time, will always be sufficient.

Happiness is sometimes found in writing. Not because you can play with words, but because, ones truest feelings are never a game.

The greatest of men can speak the wisest words, but those not considered great, can demonstrate the greatest wisdom.

Some people specialise in one area, and some are awoken by many. But few, understand the power of love, and the many doors it opens.

The wise will know when to speak and when not to. But the brave will speak the truth, when others think it is not so wise. This makes, truth, the wisest at the right moments.

When one has overcome the pressures of life, through understanding the reality they have been placed in, then the realities many others see, can change.

There have been many people that have changed this world. But there have been many more people who have made this change happen.

Technology would not be the cause for negative consequences if people stopped using their mind. But it would be the lack of progress within technology.

A long explanation can sometimes bring forth too many questions, but a short explanation, has the power to redefine many answers.

There are many examples in nature that demonstrate a non physical connection between life forms. Yet many deny this truth wholeheartedly.

Many people have a tendency to attack those that possess something not entitled to them, and do their best to discredit that which is obvious to many more. One must learn to appreciate who they are, because there hasn't been a person, who did not have a positive place in the world, if they chose so.

Unfortunately, many are limited to the words they are able to use. Not because they don't speak the truth, but because the truth is not always easy to accept.

One should ask themselves, are they scared to challenge that which is set before them, by their surroundings, because they are scared to be different, or because they are scared not to be accepted. Neither is a good excuse, if what you are is good.

It is not about discrediting a theory. It is about not discrediting what is far too great for most to comprehend or understand.

Understanding is truly the most important factor in life. Only through it, can one understand faith, and why so many are faithless.

Dramatization has become such a norm within society, that people have forgotten the necessity of reducing friction and increasing productivity.

Admitting to a mistake is not the problem. The problem is that if the righteous admits once, they seem to be expected to admit for all that is not their fault.

Wisdom is not something that can be taught. Yet, wise traits are learned. But, one must remember, that wise words must be followed by wise thought, wise action, wise plan, and then, true wisdom is visible.

One without an emerging and blossoming soul, is one who is restricted to knowing the truth. For the soulless, anything soulful, becomes nonsense.

Sometimes to find truth, it is required to read between the lines, to read split lines, to read backwards. But, to read what cannot be read immediately, one must listen to that which does not always speak.

Confusion is the product of few. It is not the same for all, as not all confusion was designed for all. So be not confused, for that which is not directed at you. But do not shy away, of understanding the confusion surrounding you.

Without peace, how can all participate in business. Without everyone's participation, how can anything reach it's full potential.

Sanity, is not for the narrow minded. Understanding, isn't for those who can not see consequences.

Sometimes, it is necessary to fight for what appears to have no voice, before fighting for those with a voice.

Does one not wonder why there is no collective telepathy. Perhaps it is a way to protect everyone, from all that is not right in the world.

Sometimes it is necessary to fight for what has no voice, before fighting for those with a voice.

Some would say that no one uses a safety net for success. Yet, all seem to rely upon the net, for all things.

All is natural. The law of Binding All Natural Elements.

The easiest way to fight for peace, is by war. It can take decades, or a moment. But the hardest way to fight for peace, is peacefully.

Love isn't a feeling that can be learned. It's a feeling, one either has, or doesn't have. One that does, loves all things good, and fights to understand what is not. One that has no love, will make it visible by everyday actions.

To find compromise, it is hard to be compromised. But to be compromised, compromise is then hard to be found.

All things can be halted and paused. But is it wise to do the same with progress. OR is it wise, to halt those, understanding its entirety.

What is not energy but all things. How could all things exist, without energy. All energy, science seeks to understand.

Those who never forgot, will never be forgotten.

The people had always trailed far behind certain individuals, yet, all this progress was for the people.

When a virus is separated and sustained, all life begins to flourish. Yet some viruses demise begins through silence. For in silence, it spread.

Most fight for the land, sacrificing people. Few fight for the people, knowing, no land has life without them.

The rest is history, and the future is based upon it.

To believe in science, means to have an inner faith, and a desire to know, what is unknown. The same is true for all beliefs.

The greatest science, has always been the greatest reasoning.

Some require years of work to demonstrate what they believe or wish others to believe. Few, require only moments, to demonstrate, that it is not precise.

The sad reality is, there are people who appear and or are, very intelligent for many, but not so much, for a few.

Nearly all things, left behind as help, from one time to another, has always had those, who have tried to stain it, so truth is harder seen and accepted.

The only reason there seems to be no perfection in anyone, is because others will not allow for it, or try to sabotage its every moment. For this reason, it is found in self reflection.

Do not judge ones desire to see the good in everything, and truth in everything. There is a major difference, and not many can do it.

Nothing is ironic. IF you believe solely in reason. But reason, is viewed differently, and may depend on interests. Was it there to teach you, or do you claim it as the result.

Everything that was right, was always said on time.

There's one statement, that has caused confusion and fear, more than any other within life. "Keep your friends close, and your enemies closer".

When you choose to throw away perfection, you have decided on the path of decline.

With all fact and fiction re-evaluated. One would be wise to consider. Is the rebellious one still not good, and what was the rebellion over.

It is not a requirement to destroy any religion or belief system. What is necessary, is to understand their purpose and the message they send.

If one were to look past the past, and make the presence the problem. Then there is a big problem.

This democracy is much clearer and original, than the one of the decades left behind. That democracy was sold. This democracy can become the truth.

It seems easier to believe liars, as there is less to think, than to believe truth tellers, as it actually requires the mind to think.

A difference between, an individual, fighting the fight with their own mind, and one being taught, is a sign, that intelligence is from elsewhere.

How can the best be expected, when the worst is always offered.

Sympathy is a blasphemous word. Symphony is a natural remedy as its substitute. Simplicity, unites them both.

In this world, and perhaps those of old, it was wisest, not to trust anyone, and do great deeds, then to trust many, and accomplish nothing at all.

Beware of services offered. Some are separately coffered.

When abandoned by anyone, in progressing for what is good for all, than the abandoned, will, continue the path alone.

Some names, never change, but people do. Some names change, but people don't. Changes occur, because the rules change. Deception is clouded.

For that which seems, cannot be proven, precise reasoning, has always sufficed. For some things, it is the only thing necessary, if precise.

What for one is freedom, for another is oppression. To unify the difference, so all understand the meaning of both, time was always required.

There are those, who are encouraged to take a break, without consequences. Then, there are few, that simply can't, because of consequences.

The wrong people, too many times, are given the right to simple gifts within life, and the right people, are placed in a state, to feel that these rights, are wrong.

To fight what is natural, in feeling, and to fight what is unnatural, is not a fight many are faced with, in such a high degree.

Requiring the need, to justify wrongdoing, by causing more wrongful action, is proof of wrong, and precedents or contracts, therefore become void.

Once capacity increases, so does understanding, so does re-evaluation, so does belief, then reduces fear, and allows for good things to reach all.

A better future, cannot be, without a corrected past.

To steal from the world, is never excusable.

There is no possibility of making anything great, by removing what is able to propel it forward.

If people learned to view cultures and beliefs, as entities protecting certain truths, and not as opponents of any truth, unity would be simplified.

Never too late to realise collectively, mistakes that have been made. Only because one who didn't make them, never gave in. All else is too late.

Belief is feeling and understanding, of what defies logic, cannot always be explained. Any intelligence that hits a wall, learns what belief is.

A pre determined agenda, will not allow for what is being told, to be heard. For if it was heard, then what was being prepared, would not have been said, or put into practice.

Each situation, is governed by laws, of what is known as a case to case study. It is based, on psychology, of what is thought and or, then said.

It's hard, for those stooping low, to fly high. But those flying high, will easily see those, stopping low. For the heights of those flying high, are untouchable.

Not all can be grateful for what occurs, for not all are equipped, to understand that which is occurring. But some eyes, have never let go.

A library can be complete even with one book, if it is precise in all aspects of life.

Some work a number of hours, for a certain amount, to satisfy their needs, which is not a problem. Yet few, never stop working, so that many more others, are able to.

It takes a negative scenario, to actually understand consequences. Yet saving from such scenarios, positively, consequences are not seen.

It is in itself evident, in those who wish to pull the strings of other peoples lives, who they are, and those that seek to fight for freedom.

Limited capacity, will not allow, to look up, or to see far. It will go down a blinded road, with false expectations. After all, it is limited.

After creation, some of the greatest things ever accomplished, are those things that did not happen. This is to say, negative actions were prevented.

One cannot dirty the neighbours yard on one side, and clean the neighbours yard on the other side, and state, that they have done a good deed.

It is the reaction that can draw something closer, that did not know, the intention was always so.

Early simple teachings, do not lack explanation. But those who understand, realise, that it took explanatory science, to fill in the details.

They who delete truth and past, delete themselves.

A Shepard guides his flock, and does not control his flock.

There is no truth greater, than that, of truth not being accepted.

Among many and all things that have helped save the world as is known to most. It is tears, that have made all this possible, and the impossible, only natural.

Frequencies plenty, but for the majority frequency is tuned, but like all things, frequency can be translated. Yet only few, know this too.

The most beautiful moment's, can be when ones mind is relaxed, and no tension or judgment is placed upon thought. The hardest, is not being able to. Which then requires new methods, based upon surroundings.

Few see the mind in its entirety. Most see the outer portion, allowing for a calmer life. This in itself, makes it more difficult for those few who see its entirety.

To know what awaits the next few moments, via technological communication, is advancement brought by few for many. To know without, is a gift to all.

When all the burden is placed upon one, then all endure the consequences. When many share the burden, than consequences become very minimal.

If one must fight monsters, when they arise, than rely upon the outcome. But if all worked together, monsters would never have existed.

It was the branding of the word telepathy, and the preservation of what one would describe as Greek knowledge, that united beliefs, into a more unified world.

It is better to care too much for what is righteous and for all, than to care for the wrong things in any moment.

It's those who care, that will be demonised, for the momentary lapse in which they say they don't care, and rarely, those who have never cared.

A clean cloth, may at times be used to soak up what is unclean, but can always be washed clean.

The need to trick, betray, lie, deceive, play games, manipulate, cause pain, to a child, all through life, is a sign of complete inferiority.

The world was for too long being affected by what others said, and did not hear what was actually being said.

One who can think, write and speak in a manner unknown to all, even thought from the same individual, for some reason, is perceived as different sources, yet its the same individual.

Discretion in the wrong few words, tangles many wrists. Yet, time reveals, the tangled wrists, should have been the ones given discretion.

What is good, will forever remain good. Yet, through time, all that is not, will do its best, to attach, the opposite, out of spite and jealousy.

A true face always reveals itself. A dream is not just a dream. A vision is not just a vision, and a revelation, is shown in many forms and ways.

There's a misconception, of what drops, must have fallen. But existence, is full of surprises. Such as one rising, that chose to initially jump.

Everyday, in this form of life, one or more come to the realisation of a greater reality. Yet only one realises, they had always known it.

It is a sad truth, that only after mistakes upon another, or after they are no longer amongst others, is it truly realised, what was amongst them.

You will notice, by which another places their time and effort into, of what they think and what they are capable of. That is what they'll offer, forever.

There is the thought, and the idea, that there are many elements, which differ in property and form. Yet, one who understands, knows, it's all one.

Time is just an illusion, and the delusion, is based on time.

Limits, are for those, who only see the near future. The limitless, is only for those that see infinite.

Energy put forth, by the power of the mind, stronger than all in its path, isn't only an extension of that mind, but an everlasting presence.

Truth never dies, but due to choices, not everyone gets to see its entire true beauties and wonders.

One must understand, by simple analogy. A painting may not be perfect in everyones opinion and in all detail. But if it were destroyed, even the beauty would be gone.

Some minds, take upon entire new dimensions, that accusations, become standard, even by those minds, claiming to be brighter than all others.

There are some things that can't be taken back, and the worst of those things, are when they were based upon things that never were.

To require food, is the same as saying, to need food. To want food, is understandable, as one both requires food, and needs food to live.

A saying yet to be said, but one that will last as long as conscious life. "A fact, can be just a thought". For it was the will, before it was a word.

You cannot know something, if you rely upon another for it to be done. You cannot be someone, if you rely upon the one who is that someone.

A trick and deception can feed a small party. A global plan accompanied by countless ideas, can feed everyone. The world has too many times chosen the first.

Some never give up, for the right reasons. Some for the wrong. But it's the ones who don't give up for the wrong reasons, that eventually, learn the hardest.

One must be willing to learn, if they are to be taught.

Life cannot be an adventure, if there are no obstacles.

The truth has always been within. Yet only let out, can many others, share in its ugly and enlightening beauty.

To be ones own master, is what no master can teach another.

Not all will be honoured for their noble life and deeds for others. But if one only lives for such rewards, than their deeds, were never as stated above.

Majority find it a burden, carrying their own pain through memories and thoughts. Yet imagine, those who carry those of others. Their own simply become a lesson, for others, and those of others, the pain of not being able to change the outcome prior to its happening.

All mountains breath, but some have extra lungs.

All that is here, one way or another, came from the sky.

The groundwork had been completed, and the knowledge collected from far and wide. Yet still, the only way to combine it all, was to add the right angles.

Stories can travel long distances, and truths can be retold as myths, lies may become the norm for many, but with correct actions, all becomes as was meant to be.

Thoughts and actions, are the beginning of laws and reactions. For one can act blind to their presence, but all are or will become aware of their existence.

If it happened, it's a fact, and memorised within existence. Irrelevant, whether it can be explained or not, through an individuals level of knowledge or understanding. But all things are one day explained.

Your own actions, determine your own present, and therefore, your own future.

The one who created the lie, will be the one who feeds the information. The one who was the subject of the lie, will be the one who works it out.

When one occupies their mind, setting another up, that is all they know. When one is always learning, than you never know, how much they actually know.

The truth only hurts those, that have denied it, for their entire lives.

One who is strong, can never be broken of their will or spirit. But their desire, or choice, will change direction, depending on all others.

It's easy to see beauty in anything, when the ugliness is scattered. But able to see the beauty, when surrounded by ugly, isn't easy.

All children are born good, but not all adults are. There arrives a stage, when the children either adopt what surrounds them, or fight for good.

The wrong actions, can cause the best possible future, not to unfold.

One who has seen a lesser reality, cannot know of life, in the same way, of one who has witnessed a greater reality. For their truths differ.

For small minds, great ideas and much larger plans, will always be deemed, delusional and grandiose.

Why should change be asked of those, who have done good.

Major corruption is only possible through a process of thought, installation of information, and manipulation of memories. The opposite is also true, but must be fought for.

Stupidity is a sign of unawareness. Unawareness is a sign of not knowing what is, and what is to be.

Some have the capacity to stay out of the limelight, and continue their cruel ways, whilst some refrain, until the opportunity is there again.

What is said now, was once said. The only difference is, the age it was said in, and the aftermath, upon which only few believed it was true.

One word has many letters, but only two directions. It's letters that make up words, and some people that make what is good, appear bad. This is evidence of lack of knowledge and the truth.

There is no hope, for the hopeless. There is no future, for those who cannot see the true past.

The one challenge, few dare to take on, is the one making life better, for those who have no choice, and those who's choices are being made hard everyday.

There is no greater cost, than the one you do not know you have made.

Not to be prejudice, is one among many things, that allow for great things to occur, and great plans to unfold.

Words have the potential to be abused, and its forthcoming energy, may confuse many. But true ideas, combined with planning and correct application of code or numbers, will only provide a closer realisation of purity, that has been avoided in the words themselves.

What stays pure, stays true. Even in the visual world, surrounding all.

Some battles are fought alone. Those fighting such battles, battle for all those who are, and are not alone, but cannot, understand the fight. It is they, that pay for their own battles, so the majority can be left alone.

For the unrelenting will, there is no such thing as gravity, or impossible. All that there is, is the need, to find a way, that it all works.

Not all forms of energy that are harnessed, are visible, neither to the naked eye, nor to any known, or unknown, technology.

It's no secret, that with all special interests, there must be winners, losers, or hard compromise. But there's always a way, that any loss, is never felt.

True strength, is not using all of ones power, if the need is not existential.

The eternal good, knowledgeable, insightful, truthful, understanding, caring, and force in existence, will not help, if there is no need.

One only knows, what nobody else knows, because they are a part of it.

There have been many who have searched for the source of secrets and wonders. Unknowingly it was amongst. But for choices, very little was actually revealed.

Growing up, and seeing only the beauty in the world, and then realising all truths no one else could see, brings upon a desire at times, not to believe that it is true, even though, such reality, hides from no one.

The fight to remove the thorn from the majority, only places more upon thyself. Yet the thorn, was never placed by the one removing it.

The majority of society is quite sane, that's why selective few are used for certain objectives. Intelligence and sanity are not one the same.

Played into the hands of a few, who seek to control, and really, only one always stood in their way of complete destruction. Thus, never allowing for destruction to occur.

Some mistakes can only be made once, and some cannot be made at all. When those that can't be made, are made, only miracles can rebalance it all.

Like an air bubble in the vastness of the ocean, waiting to meet its destiny, in the vastness of the atmosphere.

Memories once many sought to destroy, become the very basis, of what many then fight for, to regain.

There is a clear difference when the help, through letters and numbers, is pure and clear, and when it is manufactured to create the opposite.

There is nothing that cannot be explained. The problem is, who's ready to accept the truth, and who's doing everything to sabotage the truth.

To be able to solve a problem, one must find either the original source, or the original mechanisms used. Only then, is the problem much clearer.

Never compare loses. For each suffering, cannot be measured the same way.

Follow the mind, don't follow only words. But if you cannot read the mind clearly, then stick to the words. For energy, has many components.

A truth seeker, or holder of truth, is someone, who must teach others, as it was their purpose, but were not taught, exactly what to teach, when particularly, surrounded by misinformation.

Public morality, either taught of old or new, will always stand the test of time. For what ever has stood between humanity, morals saved the day.

A show of immorality can only feed a limited few, for a limited time.

The only reason perfection doesn't exist amongst humanity, is because there are too many that wish to destroy anything even close, for their own imperfect, satisfaction.

You can't stop people thinking, and the amount of energy built through large numbers thinking alike or similar, can cause suffering, but also heal, if understood.

For any or anything to live, first there must be space.

He who understand it all, was always a part of it all.

There is only one word for intelligence in every language, and for is it not true, that only few seek intelligence their lives.

Faith has no boundaries, religion does.

Traitors always live inside the nation.

For every truth, there is a lie, and for every lie, there is a truth.

Some stories would truly be beautiful, if they weren't so ugly.

Some pain destroys all within its radius, and some pain, believes, that all within can learn, and be what is hasn't been yet.

Actions of individuals, will always differ from those of the groups they relate to. Therefore, one cannot be associated with the other.

There is a world apart, between growth and maturity of intelligence, and that of emotions.

A farm may have rough terrain, but it has no speed humps.

The large amounts of words, was there to show two types of people. Those who simplify it, for use of intelligence, and those who remind us, of none.

It is easier for many to help one, than it is for one to think for many.

One cannot be taught to think, even though one can be taught.

One can mix and match all things and put together a scribble. This is done by those, who could not put together the puzzle.

Those things more important, must sometimes wait, because that which is less important, has been given the right of way.

Numbers did not create life, yet their description through words, gives life a meaning. When meaning is taken away, than numbers mean very little.

Rule of sound, and rule of law. Lash whips, yet wipes not off the blood, but spills it. Cloth will soak up the blood.

All languages have a name, but all letters are angles.

The illusion of being free, and the reality of awareness.

When many benefit, from the work of one, than they never did it for themselves.

Light switched on, and down it shined, the centre source, to be it lined, to help all good, so be it signed, to brighten up, for one to find.

Such a life, was always intended to try and be perfected.

If one must suffer, than there's a lesson to be taught, and there's no one better to teach such lesson, than the one that has suffered.

Not everything we see, we always wanted to see, yet, we must.

It is difficult approaching, or dealing with an individual, that loves no one, but only loves things.

Oath of silence applies in many cultures, in many forms. Yet it seems, truth is that which is silenced, unless useful for abuse, and lies that which is communicated, to further abuse, or drown out the truth.

All that is, is known.

Symbolism, itself is a story. One cannot include themselves, if intending to delete the story.

Less is made, if more is destroyed.

One must not always remove something, to enhance its performance. Sometimes, it is simply necessary to add.

Letters have a numerical value, but the numbers, also have an opposite.

Working outside the scope of traditional time, is a bonus, only when others follow, and pay attention.

To have others gain and benefit from another's suffering, and the one suffering, is required to correct all mistakes, is mission impossible.

A simple mind cannot provide more feedback than what has been offered. No matter how much one searches, there is no other compressed information.

No one was ever taught how to justify their own suffering. Particularly, when they cannot find the wrong, but were punished as if it were real.

Winning something, is not the same as earning something. In saying that, there are many who deserve to win.

A negative presence of any energy, is not superior. If understood, identified and aware of, one will not be affected by it.

The word came after the thought.

All words, are accompanied by correct sayings, and moral laws, in all languages, so to never be abused or corrupted.

When the shortest stick, is given to the one with the furthest reaching abilities, it may just be that one, that cuts themselves off.

There can never be a better life, if the majority, don't try to improve upon it. More importantly, is distinguishing, that which is good, and that which is not.

It is better to be homeless, than to be a slave. Not all slaves must build pyramids.

When the fight is over something unknown to the one the fight is over, then the story is never what is being told, and possibilities diminish.

The money cannot be made before the idea.

The body is different to the mind, only if the mind is not aware of the body. For the body, cannot always move, where the mind can.

Seems correct applying the first visible syllable to a word. Creating unnatural consequences. So one must read within, to change the outside.

A quick dialogue requires as simple information as possible. Yet, if misused too much, the advanced truth within, can be lost if not taught.

There is nothing that cannot be made sense of. The catch is, not all things should be made sense of, and those things that should, should not be avoided.

All things are present. Not all things have a clear picture attached initially. As the air flows all ways, and cannot be captured in one frame or as one, so too, understanding presence, must be understood separately, before being understood as one.

To rely upon oneself for all matters, and having the only guidance being that of sense, takes one, to places beyond the visual scope, not many others can understand.

The truth never lies.

All things are known, but not to all.

When truth is subdued, and lies pushed forward, one must be careful what they become, and what they make of life itself.

If you seek to destroy something good, only to use it how you see fit, it can never be or become, what it was meant to be.

A dream is only a dream, when it has no relevance to reality. A living dream, can be a nightmare, until fulfilled.

Some things, are worth a lifetime of sacrifice, knowing good can be seen, however far away it may be. Yet, some things, aren't worth the same.

Belief has no language barrier or border. Belief is mostly determined by vision, yet few see it everywhere.

Some tracks are left in writing, and for those few, the rest are immortalised in memory.

Understanding is amongst the most vital characteristics in order to know reality. Yet, some things, few can actually completely understand.

It is better to feel sorry for oneself, than expect others to feel sorry. Yet, sympathy and compassion, are not the same as feeling sorry.

Some things switch on, and some never switch back on again. One must be wise, to know which one is more important to apply.

If the messenger initiated, contributed or continued the problem, they are no longer just a messenger, of anyone or anything.

To be taught a lesson, by those who had created the problems, is no different, than being resuscitated by those who drowned or strangled you.

To neither have what one wants or what one needs, yet to accomplish what one must, is not an easy task.

Bricks can only be layered, level by level. Requiring order and sequence.

No plan is worth the value stated, if communication is polluted. Thus, making language, as fundamental, as the economy itself.

At times, there are battles going on in the world, so to only protect the life inhabiting it. Such battles, are rarely known, or understood.

If the light is visible, than it is there and is no lie.

To feel what others feel, and yet, for none other, to understand what one feels, is as difficult as loving the world, but not everyone within it.

To love the world, but not everyone in it, is a difficult experience.

What is complicated for most, can prove to be incorrect, and what appears most complicated, supported by rules, can be proven to be very simple.

There are things, all know of as negative consequences, or domino affects. But there're also, rarely used, positive domino affects.

Not all that is old is bad, and thus has been brought into the present, but the present, has brought much new, bettering things of old.

Some things require contracts to determine accountability, access, control etc. Yet, few things, simply require a good intended mind.

The simple difference between old and new. Once, the law was the word. Today, many confuse the law and word, with the sword and path.

There is a difference to simply read a lot, without understanding its meaning, and to read little, allowing for the mind to expand its meaning, and understand its fullness.

There're options of correcting the present, or starting again. Yet if one doesn't learn how to correct the present, starting again is pointless.

You cannot draw parallels, or understand what is happening, or what has happened, if you do not think calmly and sensibly.

Someone who is working for a better future, does not try and destroy the present.

Some mistakes at forced upon, and others are made, because something is not understood.

No one can escape life, once they exist.

It wasn't a crazed man feeding the pigeons. It was confused individuals, who didn't see its purpose.

It is an unnecessary negative application of psychology, to separate any group within society, as all groups are formed from and by the people.

It's good to manage and understand all things, it's just difficult, when one has to do it all themselves.

It's difficult to see what no one else can see simultaneously, still, it is much easier, when understood what's been seeing, and what is happening.

Cradle of civilisation is not based on a place, but where the people who share its entire truth, are situated.

If the mind is aware, the body can be anywhere.

One may not be able to experience all that another does, making it appear unrealistic. But applying intellect, and reasoning, the truth can be made a lot clearer for all others in appearance, by way of thought.

Many specialise in different areas, yet without understanding all sections, the proper, and correct solutions, can be hard, to be put into force.

All written languages, are their own form of hieroglyphics. The exception is, its ability to provide meaning, and to continue the story of life.

It's not the same to have the ability to adapt to ones surroundings, and to respect ones surroundings. Adaptation, can include forced change, and respect, is followed by integration.

Science is one form of understanding matters, present in everyday life. Such area, should not be taken for granted, or mistaken for taking over.

The only difference between any life form, is the state in which that life is situated, or based in.

Only by understanding something, can one defeat, yet defeat, does not always mean destroying something, but can also mean exactly this.

It's a waste of time trying to change the world, yet making it better, is worth every bit of effort.

Someone will look at the sand, and see just sand, while someone else, will see a castle.

The introduction of letters, has been one of the greatest advancements for people, as it has provided the basis for understanding elements of beginning.

Life itself, is a testament, to how much all rely upon others, to advance.

A number will correspond to multiple meanings, yet its most precise, and true reason, is not easy to find or accept, if polluted with prior misinformation.

Multiple dimensions, or thought, by way of quantum physics, begins, with language.

A psychological agenda, through positive/negative propaganda, never occurs without, other agendas, promoting separate causes simultaneously. One must recognise, whether it is for better or for worse.

It's difficult to create an enclosure, unaffected by outside negativity, yet once achieved, it's much easier to influence outside positively.

Experts make the money, and money, pays for the experts.

Correct psychological observation, of anything, is an accomplishment, few have ever achieved.

The best coincidences, are those intended.

There's a difference between a painting from the heart, and one from the mind. A poisoned heart, will demonstrate its intentions via a poisoned mind, through its actions. Initially, unaware to many, yet through time, obvious to all.

It is easier to put together what is not broken, yet, it is much harder once it is broken. If accomplished in such instance, than nothing is too hard to put together.

Some realities, are hard to imagine by many, only because they do not accept it on time.

Fair trade, is only at times possible through what would appear as unfair actions. For if one hadn't endured such actions, more would possibly be unfair.

By refusing to do what is wrong, one has already freed them self more than the one who does. Consequences may hurt for the one who refuses, yet eventually, less will hurt generally.

The saddest statement in life, is perhaps, "I told you so", the second saddest is perhaps, "Don't do it that way, do it this way". Neither is rewarding.

Everything was perfect. Yet with corrupted individuals, not even perfection is good enough, only because it does not go their way. Therefore, the fight is against such individuals.

Taking into consideration only the welfare of others before oneself, makes it hard to expect a positive return, and if not recognised, can cause one to forget themselves also, even though the effort was for others.

There are simply levels of the mind few can truly understand. As such, many choose to play upon the level they are at, creating immeasurable problems.

Sometimes, things simply don't get easier, one just has to become stronger. Not all is always known, when one or many require to know them on time.

It is good to listen to everything surrounding one, yet it is absolutely not good to accept it all.

There's a clear distinction, between loving something more, than hating something. By hating, it eventually crawls right into itself, making it visible to all.

Each letter corresponds to another, as do words, and applied binary. Since words have more letters, more meanings apply, as do messages within.

It's difficult creating a system that works. Yet what can be more difficult once in place, is demonstrating its correctness and necessity for all.

As time is perceived, it cannot be slowed down. Yet thoughts defying time, can demonstrate slowing down time, if entire thoughts are broken down.

When large tasks are being put together, one becomes agitated, at unnecessary inconveniences, let alone those brought upon intentionally. This can be viewed both positively and negatively.

Most individuals who create problems, aren't aware of the consequences. This is solely due to their understanding of the reality surrounding them.

Expectation is a false emotion, if it's purpose is of incorrect judgement.

It is the sense of life, that allows for one to travel into the unknown, seeking life, that is beyond their visual scope. For after all, it is the goodness of life, that seeks the goodness of life in all things.

What is basic for one, may be advanced for another. Understanding this, actually helps understand much more.

Syllables can be connected to any word. Therefore creating false versions of meaning. If one is forced to overlap the truth, a negative psychological presence can occur if not countered by the truth and precise reasoning and explanation.

Awareness, is a force of its own.

Nothing is too big to fail. The true interpretation or attached meaning should be though, that anything great designed to help, should never be given up on.

One should never generalise any group or name. For what is good, can be forced to appear, and therefore become known in the same negative context as it's true opposite.

It is as easily said, as is to be done. For it is through both precise and imprecise sayings, that all things are done thereafter, and onwards.

Individuals find hard escaping a negative whirlpool, caused by only a few individuals, yet the difficulty level rises, when continued by many more.

If the purpose of any is to corrupt another, others must apply this version for defence, therefore leading all to such a negative state unknowingly. This must be countered always on time.

What's simple, requires simple maintenance. Yet, what is of great design and complexity, will therefore require same attention in maintaining.

No one should ever let go, of what none other can do.

Some minds have the capacity, to outdo, even their own.

If one is forced to understand and learn what is wrong, than it is only just, for any other, to have to learn, and listen, to what is right.

As energy of existence is immortalised, so too, is its memory.

There have been times, that if truth was told or accepted, the path would have been clearer. As lies preceded upon one another, truth became less clear.

There is no such thing as a clash of cultures, if all relied upon one another for their advancements.

If one plays on emotions, they may never receive intelligence, and yet if one applies intelligence, without feelings, they may never find sense.

How can advanced progress be made, if not even written language is understood properly, and spoken form is not used correctly.

Cultures, languages and belief systems, teach a proper path, when united correctly. To see right, than one would know the importance of all birth.

One would be surprised what damage a few individuals could do to the world, and still, one would be more surprised, what one could do, to repair it all.

If captains cannot read the map, all go the wrong way. That is why captains should be chosen wisely, and advice should be taken sincerely.

In a state of confusion, most will believe in any information. That is why confusion is created, so true information, is hard to be reached.

The feeling one can have from truth, itself is an indication that all great things were intended by some, to be corrupted. What is left then, is to simply find it.

An equation is written in its most simple forms, yet describes most complex things for most. So too, a sentence can appear very simple.

If an area, has a million rocks, it does not offer a million possibilities, for each rock can be thrown in infinite directions and places.

It's either broken down properly, so that it works, or it's not broken down at all.

Learn the angles, learn the scripts, apply the methods.

It is better for either all to be intelligent, or all to lack it, but be good. Yet, it is best, to be wise and good.

Faith is not for the faint hearted.

Place someone in the wrong profession, and the returns become minimal.

Reality is greater than an area just one may specialise in. Therefore, realities differ. Not because of existential reality, but understanding its entirety.

Maybe not everyone can be saved how we wish, at the right time or right way. But if we don't try when its known to be required, then it's a fail.

If one was to simply read the hour clock as it was intended, all things since its inclusion, would have turned out, much more positively.

Everything is encrypted. To what degree, that is yet fully unknown.

There's a difference between falling and jumping. It's called a choice. Those who fall unjustly, are caught, and those who jump, will try to catch others.

All things were once pure if understood, and all things are hybrid if observed correctly, and freedom was fought for all, but not by all.

The only way one could create an overlapping map, that appears as the true path, is to remove the majority of the truth, making one believe in the lie.

As earth has become smaller in way of communication and connection, so too has it become larger in the world itself. This brings along change.

If the majority new the truth, surrounded by a false version, it would affect their own belief, let alone, if the majority believed in the lie itself.

Even if one knew everything, they wouldn't be able to share it in a single human lifetime.

Intelligent design, was such, that intelligence and goodness can never disappear or dissipate. It is eternal as existence itself.

Future is present.

The pages of written philosophy and psychology, are ones that can never be completed, as it is an ever evolving basis of life, based upon ever evolving situations and occurrences. Using applied psychology therefore, is difficult even for specialists.

It's everywhere and in everything. If viewed directly, lesser results will appear. If viewed with a greater scope, all details become more prevalent.

Its natural to apply hearing senses, to determine ones accent, by voice, through the magnitude of alternating currents, travelling by air.

A sample allows and shows more room in awe the directions.

One can never pop a bubble if it is beyond their reach.

Half an answer, only gets you half way there. Yet some, may know how to use even a sixth, to get the entire answer.

Even the highest of things, can be brought into a lowly state. This is not necessarily, a negative.

The world isn't silent, and it is not only one individual thinking or speaking.

There are countless roads. Yet if the same one is being told repeatedly, than all begin to believe it is the only one.

If there was such a thing as fate, then fate can appear as a delusion, if it isn't told right.

To know, but to not accept, only to believe it is not true, is the same as allowing for the same negativity, to repeat itself over and over again.

Spoken language, differs from coded language.

Reduction of advancement, can begin with a single phone call. The increasing of advancement, occurred when making the right call.

Most things, build a bridge. But, is it one, you wish to cross.

Do not ever believe your own lies, even if perfected.

The warrior stands on guard, waiting for the dragon.

Corrupted coding in a program is initiated from outside, yet, corrupted coding within an individual, is self inflicted, via lack of knowledge.

When one statesman cannot match the goodness or greatness of another, the only way to become recognisable, is in the opposite direction.

The truth is hidden, so that it cannot be corrupted, and revealed only, when the time is right.

No program can work without the computer.

The source of life can never be broken. But its presence amongst humanity, can disappear, as a result of actions caused within humanity.

It is not those who see goodness, which are larger in number that choose to voice the truth, but those who can't think, have benefit from wrongdoing.

Even a spiders web must be organised. That's not to say, or intend of thinking of it as a trap, but even with a negative connotation, positivity can be extracted.

Energy can in a certain way be explained like the ocean water. If one is in cooler waters, they cannot see the warmer waters, but can feel it approaching.

Some languages cannot be spoken, but all languages can be explained.

Not all seek to see what must be seen in the right time, and many seek for it not to be seen within a certain time, or not at all. But all see, within time.

The amazing inclusion of rules and perfection of language, has yet to be demonstrated by any individual. Once this occurs in its complete form, corrections will begin to appear more suddenly.

Not everyone has the luxury, of saying they did nothing wrong, without having to explain. Hard part is, explaining what another did wrong.

If all read, write and speak in the language they were born into, and translators were used only to interpret another, no vulgar similarities would be known to any.

Perfection can never be corrupted on an existential level. Yet among humans, even perfection, is sought to be corrupted.

When it happens, no one has the right to say, they didn't know. Cause it's not happening, no one seems to say, what if it does.

Destroying anything that is great or contributes to what is great, with intention of introducing, ones own version of greatness, actually destroys all greatness.

Difficulty is not seeing good or bad. Difficulty is seeing the good and bad in everything.

The awareness, creatures on earth, have for their natural surroundings, is an intelligence, that is given too little credit or acknowledgement.

If a rock older than earth itself, arrived to earth now, even though arriving last, it was still before. This rule applies to many wonders.

Not all written languages are sedentary.

All know what they do, but not all know the consequences of what they are doing.

Simple language was designed to do good. Yet, if such simplicity is corrupted, than advanced language, becomes harder to learn or accept.

If one thought 3 times, after measuring twice, perhaps they would not have to cut, but realise joining, is the correct method.

For something to even begin to work on a global scale, it cannot be corrupted. Before biological life, all things must have had to be perfected, for life itself to exist and continue.

The earth was never a mixed puzzle. It was put together perfectly. The problem was, and is, someone is trying to destroy the masterpiece.

To have and to learn two scripts, via 1 language, shows truths, hard to find, in only one script.

Corruption begins through language, for it is after all, what the majority rely upon, affecting everyday psychology and actions.

Nothing was made to be broken apart, and abused or misused. Everything that is to be broken apart, was to be put back together for the better.

It's good to know oneself, but it's also good to know those around.

There is no back door for all things. But if one is inside, than why should they search for an exit, or such a door.

From everything, one can learn something, but not everything, teaches, something intelligent.

Mountain, shared the word.

Word, shows, the road.

Change is not change. Same is not same.

Sometimes, an updated version of a script, requires its original form or forms, to show all of the rules accompanying it.

The study of short phrases sufficing, is perhaps more insightful, than its elaborating counterpart.

When one defends a nation or entity, knowing it is part of the global good, one can not look at what is not good within it. For one either defends, or does not.

One must apply only a few actions in such a negative manner, for much goodness to be misread, and for many to stay misinformed.

Standard intelligence is destroyed through improper use. The problem therefore, isn't teaching high intelligence, but that it is capable of becoming abused if not incorporated properly.

The most complex written forms of language, aren't exactly the most complex.

Lines, curves and dots, are the essential signs for all written languages.

There is but one truth. Yet, to save all that is good, the entirety will never be known to all. For this, one must be aware of all the lies.

Everyone's wish was knowing the truth. Yet only one wished to save the truth. Overtime, lies connected to truth. Making the wish a hard to get truth.

It is easier to say, seek and you will find, but it is harder to look, for what you must see.

As all are forms of energy, possessing information, than imagine the information stored within the energies surrounding earth itself, and beyond.

Sometimes throwing out a theory filled with 'intelligence' is easier to bare, than it is to accept a truth one cannot always understand, even though, each puzzle, fits perfectly, and without ill teaching.

A dream can occur as ones eyes close, or just before waking. There is no rule. Each moment as real as life. Portraying reality, in a manner, to understand life.

One doesn't need to be payed to think, for all were given a brain to use.

For 'innocent' perpetrators, attack had been the best defence through life. But when used for all actions, the truth reveals itself slowly.

One will write in a pronunciation version, removing true identity, and the other writes in its correct form, yet not applying proper script, making both wrong.

The dictionary, hasn't been decoded, and as such, has been coated, not for what it is, or for what's being said, yet in time, all will see it re-ad.

One must first know and see the true nature of philosophy, science and all applicable laws, to understand systems of belief, and consequences thereafter.

It doesn't matter which language one speaks or writes in, for the meaning is all the same, if one understands the purpose of the letters and words.

If people were more proud of their own languages, the beauty of all things would be seen, by all.

All roads lead to the same destination.

All was made, and the same still exists in one form or another, for good reason.

Writing on paper, is a minor form of extra dimensional visualisation. Yet allows to see the most complex forms, therefore only limited by an individual.

You cannot steal what you don't see. You cannot use, what you do not understand.

Listening is not always a recommended skill. Observing and understanding can alter this, at times, a corrupted form of learning.

One cannot be equipped for life, if upon them is placed a false version of life.

An alternate version, with corrupted elements all the way through, not only affects those it's implemented into, but those implementing it.

Applying this one angle correctly, beginning slowly, all will fall into place. It is called the lioness.

One must remember, to deter a child, and educate what is right, writing must be styled.

The truth is a lot more beautiful than a lie. The reality is though, it must be hard for one or a few, before it is beautiful for all the rest.

The unit always stays the same, upside up, or upside down, and the only thing that alters, is the dow, or the dot.

Central it stands, but not for all places, west it leads, to teach the spaces, southern and east, add more faces, every word, another replaces.

English was broken, then joined together, people by name, yet angles by letter, and languages unites, for what can be better.

To speak it's easy, moving straight, yet leaving crumbs, leaves the bait, so every word, must relate, to the laws, of its natural state.

It is hard to learn, and to accept, for what you're taught, seems pre-set, but applying methods, one cannot forget, roll the poll, and be old you get.

Learn your abc's and 123's, so the future won't be terminated you see, one two show and three don't try, I looked and saw I with my eye.

There is no greater way to divide, minimise intelligence, separate, destroy, reduce progress, remove civility, than by simple generalisation.

Good to listen, good to hear, good to know, year upon year, but not all thoughts, or rather what passes through, is a choice, or even true.

Add up, add down, app across, app town, see straight, see back, look way, look stack, tack cat, take k-9, took steal, took sign.

It's in the code. Flip it, turn it, spin it, straighten it, it's all the same, if you see the education.

To prey on oneself, to help many, is a prayer never told.

You is not me, but from angles and distance, you try be me, people don't see, me is me, and you is me, so they try spin me, for what suits to be you.

To truly see awe angles and views, is to truly be self enlightened. But as such, all things seek what it saw, see.

The traitor is the one who destroys what is good about their own identity, and not the one who fights by all means, to restore the good.

There is no such thing as an innocent messenger, who is willing to partake in an event, known to them, as malevolent.

When one learns to love, they learn the mind, learn to teach, what is kind, but the ill, will force what's wrong, and try create, a different song.

Awareness, is a force of its own.

It is rare, for one who is bringing you loses, to admit their place within the frame of things.

Only a sane individual, can fight for their own sanity.

One can apply silly syllables to a word, or understand that syllables themselves, detail a more intelligent application.

One can have all existence fighting for them, but in the end, if that individual doesn't fight for themselves, than it is of no use.

There are two vvays to p/\ay myth swords. The write way, which is 2rue, and apps lash, or pong way, and adds little splash.

It was the donkey that saved the injured in many wars. Yet if the mind was utilised, there would be no war.

When you have nothing good to show, yet you try and represent yourself, then you have identified yourself.

The arts of sciences will be the basis for all religions, or the religion itself in the future, and faith will be its core, taking it forward.

Some sit on the fence, sniffing out which side has less visible manure. Some remove the fence, and take on what ever is set forth.

What a waste good things can appear, when surrounded by garbage.

The more, anything moving expands, the more elements it requires. Whether it be biological, or organisational.

Some futures will never be possible, as those not possible of envisioning them, were placed before those who could.

What is said now, was once said. The only difference is, the age it was said in, and the aftermath, upon which only few believed it was true.

There is a difference between a difficult life one created for themselves, and a difficult life others create for another. The scope is large.

One can not turn a blind eye, if it is blind. But one who does see, through moral understanding, can choose, not to react.

The difference between what is known in the west as a witch, and in the east as an art, is the cultural acceptance, and sharing of information.

There is no ill intended damage that cannot be reversed, and there is no ill intended definition, that cannot be redefined.

Acceptance of visible injustice, is more than just turning a blind eye.

The only thing ever being lived, is the moment. All the rest, is psychological.

Could one teach the ability to think, to those who only listen.

With no incentives, what positive results could ever appear.

It's the very thought, of believing that one can do, all & anything they please, that brings forth destabilising factors, which have the potential of creating ripples right through.

No word was designed or written to be vulgar in nature, but only to teach its correct purpose.

Understanding, can be the consequence.

Consequences, can sometimes bring forth belief, and belief, knowledge.

It is not the same, claiming what is not yours, and being given what is from another.

The pet is taught to walk up the steps, and educated, and shown, how to walk back down.

Un-rightful Credit, can be the same as plagiarism.

Livestock, should always be separated and viewed, as life first.

Endurance begins with the mind, and ends with the minds.

Sometimes it is just will, that makes the ground breaking intelligence.

A number is a tip, and not a vulgar equivalent.

To view all things existentially, possibility of infinite becomes closer.

Greed, dishonesty and betrayal, have unfortunately reshaped things, as much as being humble, truthful and loyal.

Living life based upon another, is testimony to their importance.

Just because you may be restricted biologically to seeing a minimal amount in the dark, the light is every present, in even the darkest of places.

Darkness is only a shadow.

Each one is surrounded by their own world, which is surrounded by the collective world. Only by fighting to change your inner world for the better, can one expect to change the collective world for the better also.

Not all great things are coated in diamonds. Yet, greater things produce them.

Sometimes it is important to think twice, yet, some have learned to utilise the first thought.

The pin is not kept on the pinky.

A tip, will not equate to a set up.

Opposites, always define each other.

If love was not real, than neither would exist.

One must have a humble living, to achieve less humble goals.

We don't always support what is worthy on time, but if there is still time, than supporting what is worthy, is never too late.

Never confirm anything, until the puzzle confirms itself.

Slowly go through the past, and always rush for a better future.

Sometimes we all make mistakes, because what we approach, or experience, is collectively new to all.

The least payed profession can be helping people, and the best payed, assisting people.

Some things simply, cannot be simplified. Whilst other things, only in such a way, can be understood.

Branimir BANE Maksimovic

To Be Continued....

Printed in the United States
By Bookmasters